BUSINESS ENGLISH for the Office

Karin Hirmer

Winklers

Liebe Leserinnen und Leser,

in diesem neu entwickelten Englisch-Arbeitsheft werden in abwechslungsreichen „Units" verschiedene thematische Schwerpunkte aus dem Berufsalltag von Kaufleuten für Büromanagement behandelt. Dabei geht dieses handlungsorientierte Arbeitsheft auf die moderne Berufswelt mit all ihren Kommunikationsmitteln ein. Die Verwendung einer Vielzahl authentischer „Büro-Texte" gewährleistet einen hohen Praxisbezug. Zahlreiche Aufgaben und Übungen dienen als kompetenzorientiertes Training der Fertigkeiten *Reception*, *Production*, *Interaction* und *Mediation* und richten sich somit nach den aktuellen Anforderungen der KMK.

In „First Encounter" geht es um den Einstieg ins Berufsleben; dabei auch um Themen wie Bewerbungsschreiben, Lebenslauf und Vorstellungsgespräch.
Unter dem Stichwort „Starting the Job" geht es im zweiten Kapitel rund ums Büro, um Smalltalk mit Kolleginnen und Kollegen sowie Telefongespräche.
Alles Wissenswerte zum Büroalltag findet sich unter „Doing Business" im umfangreichen dritten Abschnitt: vom Tagesgeschäft über E-Mails, Schriftverkehr und Gesprächsnotizen bis hin zu den Incoterms-Regeln.
Mithilfe des letzten Kapitels „Starting a career" erwerben die Lernenden Kompetenzen, mit denen sie im Büroberuf „durchstarten" können. Sie planen ein Meeting, erstellen eine Präsentation und vertreten ihr Unternehmen gegenüber Kunden, wobei sie interkulturelle Aspekte und geschäftliche Umgangsformen berücksichtigen. Mit dem ersten Business-Trip nach London findet „die englische Büroausbildung" einen würdigen Abschluss.

Zur Binnendifferenzierung sind alle Units in einen Basics-, einen Grammar- und einen Vocabulary-Teil untergliedert. Zahlreiche Illustrationen und Fotos lockern das Arbeitsheft auf. Der Schwierigkeitsgrad steigert sich im Laufe des Buches und die Aufgaben werden zunehmend freier.
Unter dem Hinweis „Attention!" gibt es viele hilfreiche Tipps, während die „Ideas" weiterführende Ideen bieten, wie das Englische Teil des Alltags werden kann. Neben den Anleitungen für die Rollenspiele finden sich im Büroalltag häufig anwendbare Standardphrasen im Anhang. Zudem werden die grammatikalischen Grundregeln kurz im Überblick dargestellt. Abgeschlossen wird das Arbeitsheft mit einem alphabetisch sortierten Vokabelteil zum Nachschlagen.

Ich wünsche Ihnen viel Freude und Erfolg beim Englischsprechen im Büromanagement!

Karin Hirmer

1. Auflage, 2014
Druck 1, Herstellungsjahr 2014
© Bildungshaus Schulbuchverlage
Westermann Schroedel Diesterweg
Schöningh Winklers GmbH,
Braunschweig
www.winklers.de
Druck: westermann druck GmbH, Braunschweig
ISBN: 978-3-8045-**3556**-5

First Encounter unit 1

In this unit, you will learn:

- How to apply for a job, prepare your documents and get through a job interview
- The forms of "to be" and "to have"
- The difference between the present simple and the present progressive
- To speak about dates, times and days

This is Emma Frey.
She is 19 years old.
She has just graduated as an office clerk.
She is seeking employment.
She has many interests, but music in particular.
In her leisure time she plays the guitar in a band.

She has been a volunteer for the Red Cross.

1 Find the right question word for the given answer.

1. This is Emma.	______________	is this?
2. I am from Hamburg.	______________	are you from?
3. I like the guitar.	______________	instrument do you like?
4. I'm looking for a job.	______________	are you doing?
5. I volunteer for the Red Cross.	______________	do you spend your leisure time?
6. I finished school two months ago.	______________	did you finish school?

The forms of *to be* and *to have*

	Present Simple		Past Simple	
Person	**Singular**	**Plural**	**Singular**	**Plural**
1st	I am I have	we are we have	I was I had	we were we had
2nd	you are you have	you are you have	you were you had	you were you had
3rd	he is; he has she is; she has it is; it has	they are they have	he was; he had she was; she had it was; it had	they were they had

Mit dem Hilfsverb **„to be"** (*zu sein*) bildet man alle **Verlaufsformen** (progressive) und das **Passiv** (passive); mit **„to have"** (*zu haben*) alle **Perfektformen** (perfect). Beide Hilfsverben gibt es auch als Vollverben mit eigenständiger Bedeutung, z. B.: This is nice. – He has a car.

Attention!
In der 3rd Person/Singular steht im Present Simple das Verb mit einem „s".
Im Englischen gibt es keinen Genus (der, die, das) – weiblich und männlich sind nur Personen und Haustiere.
Als Vollverb ist „to be" die Ausnahme zu vielen Regeln, z. B. dass in Fragen und Verneinungen immer zwei Verbteile stehen müssen. Für „to have" gelten diese Ausnahmen nicht.

2 **Grammar Exercise:** Fill in the right forms of *to be* and *to have* where indicated by ______________ .

Emma ________________ some time off after school. She ________________ very happy, and ________________ plans to go on vacation. She ______________________ (not, have) a car, so she decides to go to Croatia by plane. On her flight she meets a very nice couple. They ________________ from Split.

E: I __________________ Emma. Nice to meet you.

T: Hello Emma, nice to meet you. I __________________ Tomas and this __________________ Lenka, my wife. We __________________ from Split. Are you going on vacation?

E: Yes, I ___________ . Are you going home?

T: Yes, we ________________ . Do you know Split?

E: No, but I ________________ a good guide book.

L: I ___________ a few days of my holidays left, I could show you Split if you are interested.

E: That sounds great!

3 **Introducing Oneself:** Insert the correct form of "to be" where indicated by _____________ and complete the sentences (...) with information about yourself.

My name ___________ ... . I ___________ from ... . I _____________ ... years old. My hobbies _____________ ... . A special interest of mine _____________ ... .

Add information about yourself that you think might be interesting for a first encounter.

Vocabulary: Question Words

who	wer	what	was
where	wo	how	wie
which	welche, welcher, welches	when	wann

A. Job Advertisements

Wardeners are seeking an Office Clerk to work in our Merseyside Office. A good level of qualification and I.T. skills are essential, in addition to an eye for detail, an interest in patents and trademarks, excellent communication skills, and a logical and organised approach. Responsibilities include maintaining computer and manual records as well as processing of physical files and monitoring renewal deadlines.

To apply, please forward your CURRICULUM VITAE with a covering letter, including salary expectation, marked Private and Confidential to: Tracy Barker, Wardeners, Chamberlain House, Paradise Place, Birmingham, B5 2HP.

Blum Music4you KG is searching for an Office Clerk for our Munich branch. Responsibilities will include administrative duties and customer relations. Applicants must have a high school degree and have successfully completed a training/apprenticeship as office clerk. As the company language is English, our future employee should have basic English language skills. Further requirements are being computer literate and having a general understanding of administrative duties. If you want to have a career and not just a job, and are interested in the current music business, please apply enclosing your current CV to: Blum Music4you KG, Senftlstr. 8, 81541 Munich.

Emma is studying job advertisements, and she wonders how to find the right job. She wants to work for an international company or abroad, which means she will have to work in English. She divides the ads into three categories: qualifications, requirements and responsibilities.

Qualifications: Which job can I do?

German school system and a possible translation:
Hauptschule – High School
Realschule – Middle School
Gymnasium – Grammar School / Secondary School
Ausbildung – Training
Lehre – Apprenticeship
Praktikum – Internship

Attention!
The British and American school systems are very different from Germany. It is not easy to translate German schools into English, most of the time you will have to explain.

Requirements: Which job fits my personality?

Hard skills: computer literate, foreign languages, knowledge / understanding of specific areas
Soft skills: creative, communicative, open, organised

Responsibilities: Which job am I interested in?

Possible areas: administrative duties, customer relations, filing and organising daily business
Departments: purchase, sales, accounting, production, quality, maintenance

Possible departments an office clerk could apply to are:

Vocabulary

Human Resources (HR)	Personalwesen
Administration	Verwaltung
Sales department	Verkauf/Vertrieb
Purchase department	Einkauf
Accounting	Buchhaltung

35568

The simple present and the present progressive

The Simple Present

Das Simple Present wird mit dem Verb in der Grundform gebildet. Im Gegensatz zum Deutschen gibt es nur bei der dritten Person Einzahl eine andere Endung: he, she, it – das „s“ muss mit! Das betrifft also alle Dinge und Personen über die man spricht.

Person	Singular	Plural
1st	I go	we go
2nd	you go	you go
3rd	he / she / it goes	they go

Im Englischen stehen in allen Fragen und verneinenden Sätzen (mit not) zwei Verbteile. Deshalb wird im present simple das Verb „do“ ergänzt, das diese Funktion übernimmt; z. B.: I go. – Do you go? I don't go. In der dritten Person Einzahl verwendet man does. Das „s“ fällt beim Hauptverb natürlich weg, z. B.: He goes. Does he go? He doesn't go.

The Present Progressive

Das Present Progressive (auch Continuous genannt) wird mit „to be“ und der Verbendung „-ing“ gebildet. Diese sogenannte Verlaufsform gibt es im Deutschen nicht, und sie beschreibt in allen Zeitformen, dass etwas gerade oder für eine bestimmte Zeit andauert (to continue = andauern) oder einen Fortschritt (= progress) darstellt.

Person	Singular	Plural
1st	I am going	we are going
2nd	you are going	you are going
3rd	he / she / it is going	they are going

Da hier bereits ein Hilfsverb im Aussagesatz steht, wird bei der Frageform nur umgestellt:
I am going. Are you going? He is not going.

Es gibt einige Verben, die nicht im Present Progressive stehen (beispielsweise Verben, die eine Meinung einleiten), doch diese drücken auch keine Dauer oder keinen Fortschritt aus. In Handlungsketten steht ebenfalls die Simple Present Form.

4 Grammar Exercises

Emma ________________ (like) travelling. That's why she ______________________ (search) for a job with an international company. She ________________ (hope) to find a challenging job, which ______________________ (offer) opportunities for a career with the company. The Blum Music advertisement ________________________ (be) particularly interesting, as Emma ________________________ (listen) to a lot of music. At the moment she ______________________ (listen) to Hip Hop and Old School Beat, but she ___________________________ (generally, be) into all kinds of music. She ___________________________ (decide) to apply to both companies, and _________________________ (start) to work on her letter of application immediately.

> Idea:
> Find job advertisements on the Internet, e.g. on http://jobs.guardian.co.uk/ and try to find out what the requirements of the jobs are. Is there a job you would (theoretically) like to do?

B. The Application Process

Emma has decided that she wants to apply to Blum Music. She now needs to send a letter of application, a CV and references.

B.1 Writing a letter of application and one's CV: Layout and convention

Emma Frey
Zur schönen Gelegenheit 20
20359 Hamburg

Blum Music4you KG
Senftlstr. 8
81514 München

Dear Sirs

In reference to your job advertisement I would like to apply for the position as an office clerk with your company. I have recently finished my apprenticeship at Antis AG Hamburg. As you will see from my CV, I have good English and computer skills. In my leisure time I play in a band and am very interested in current music trends. I am hardworking, keen to learn and I like working in teams. I would very much like to work for Blum Music as it is an international company with great opportunities.
I hope that you will consider my application and I look forward to hearing from you soon. If you have any further questions, do not hesitate to contact me.

Yours sincerely,

Emma Frey

Vocabulary

abroad	im Ausland
administrative	Verwaltungs-
to apply for	sich bewerben um
apprenticeship	Ausbildung, Lehre
to consider	in Erwägung ziehen
current	aktuell
to hesitate	zögern
internship	Praktikum
in reference to	in Bezug auf
literate	belesen, fähig
to look forward to doing something	sich darauf freuen etwas zu tun
to maintain	aufrecht erhalten, behaupten
to monitor	überwachen, beaufsichtigen
occupation	Beruf
to process	bearbeiten, verarbeiten
recently	kürzlich
requirement	Anforderung
responsibility	Verantwortung, Aufgabenbereich
skill	Fähigkeit

355610

Europass Curriculum Vitae

Personal information	
First name(s) / Surname(s)	**Emma Frey**
Address(es)	Zur schönen Gelegenheit 20, 20359 Hamburg
Telephone(s)	040/3555362 Mobile: 0151-555789
Email	Emma.Frey@signnet.de
Nationality	German
Date of birth	24th September 19..
Work experience	
Dates	...
Occupation or position held	Internship
Main activities and responsibilities	Daily office tasks
Name and address of employer	Lieger AG, 22125 Hamburg
Education and training	
Dates	...
Title of qualification awarded	Bürokauffrau
Principal subjects/occupational skills covered	Apprenticeship as an office clerk
Name and type of organisation providing education and training	Antis AG Hamburg, vocational school
Dates	...
Title of qualification awarded	Mittlere Reife
Name and type of organisation providing education and training	Realschule (Middle School) St. Pauli, 20359 Hamburg
Personal skills and competences	
Mother tongue(s)	**German**
Other language(s)	**English**

Idea:
Go to a page where you can find the standardised Europass (e. g. http://www.europa-pages.com/jobs/europass.html) and fill out your CV in English (download), write a fake letter of application for the job you found interesting.

	Understanding		Speaking		Writing
Self-assessment / European level (*)	Listening	Reading	Spoken interaction	Spoken production	
Englisch	B1	B2	A3	A3	B2

(*) Common European Framework of Reference for Languages

Social skills and competences	Teamwork and group leader at the Red Cross
Organisational skills and competences	Organising workshops, weekly meetings and trips for the Red Cross
Computer skills and competences	Windows, Apple systems; Office software; IBM AS400
Artistic skills and competences	Playing the guitar (since 2009), lead guitar in the band "Afterthoughts"
Driving licence	B
Annexes	Diploma Mittlere Reife Reference Antis AG Training certificates Red Cross

B.2 Dealing with an invitation for an interview

Emma has received a positive answer from Blum Music.

Dear Ms Frey,

We are happy to inform you that we are considering you for the position as an office clerk. To get to know you personally, we would like to invite you for an interview. Please contact me, Meredith Williams, in the HR department to set up an appointment. My number is 089 555 785 39.

We are looking forward to hearing from you,

Meredith Williams

HR Management

Telephone Call: Emma ☎ Ms Williams

Williams: Blum Music, Meredith Williams speaking.

Emma: Ms Williams? Good morning. This is Emma Frey. I'm calling regarding the position as an office clerk. I have received an invitation for a job interview.

W: Ah, good morning Ms Frey. Yes, I've been expecting your call. Just let me look for your file ... .

E: Of course.

W: Ah, here it is. Job interviews for this position are next week, Tuesday to Thursday. Do you have any preferences?

> Attention!
> Speaking on the phone is often difficult in a foreign language, as we must rely on verbal communication only. Don't panic, but ask the other person politely to speak more slowly or to repeat something if you didn't understand it. Remember, the person on the other end of the line is also interested in communicating successfully.

E: I'll fly in from Hamburg for the day, so I would appreciate an appointment late morning or early afternoon, if this is possible.

W: Sure it is. How about Wednesday at 1 o'clock?

E: Yes, that is fine with me. Where exactly I am supposed to go?

W: You'll find directions to our company on our website. Do you have internet access?

E: Yes, I do. The address is www.music4you.de, right?

W: Yes, it is. And once you are at Blum Music, simply go to the reception and tell them you're there for the job interview. I will pick you up.

E: Great. I'm looking forward to meeting you in person, then.

W: So am I. See you on Wednesday. If you have any further questions until then, just give me a call.

E: Thanks, I will. Have a good day.

W: Good-bye.

E: Good-bye.

355612

Exercises: Present and past tense

In question tags, short answers and short agreements we use the **auxiliary verb**.

A: You like coffee, don't you? (question tag)
B: Yes, I do. (short answer)
A: So do I. (short agreement)

A: You don't like coffee, do you? (question tag)
B: No, I don't. (short answer)
A: I don't either. (short agreement)

5 Exercise

Have a nice weekend!

____

I cannot fix this.

____

I hate meetings early in the morning.

____

Have you heard? Ms Jones has been promoted!

____

I haven't got the patience to read all this.

____

And this is the purchase department.

____

Thanks for helping me out the other day.

____

I really enjoyed the conference.

____

Phrases to fill in:

So do I. – I can't either. – Same to you. – Neither have I. – You're welcome. – Me, too. – I see. – Really?

Dates

The days of the week: Monday, Tuesday, Wednesday, Thursday, Friday, Saturday, Sunday
Always with a capital letter and the preposition "on".

The months of the year: January, February, March, April, May, June, July, August, September, October, November, December
Always with a capital letter and the preposition "in".

The seasons: spring, summer, fall (US) / autumn (UK), winter
Always with the preposition "in".

> Attention!
> A date is an ordial number (1st, 2nd, 3rd, 4th, etc.), the months and the year. Watch out for 21st, 22nd, and so on. In speech, you need to add "the" at the front and "of" in front of the month. In the US, the day and the months are vice versa. If unsure, write the months in letters (Jan, Feb, etc.).

Some important holidays: Easter, Whitsun (UK) / Pentecost (US), Labour Day (1 May), Independence Day (4 July), Christmas Eve (24 Dec), Christmas Day (25 Dec), Boxing Day (26 Dec), New Year's Eve (31 Dec).
A national holiday in the UK is called a bank holiday.
Always with a capital letter and the preposition "on".

Speaking about times and days

We use the day before yesterday – yesterday – today – tomorrow – the day after tomorrow to talk about days.

We use in the morning – at noon – in the afternoon – in the evening – at night to talk about the day. Note that last night means what Germans often consider as the evening, and this morning means today's morning.

We use "to" and "past" to talk about times, a quarter and half are units that are regularly used. Note that half past nine means 9:30, and in the UK some people would abbreviate this to half nine. To avoid misunderstandings you can always say "nine thirty".
The 24 hour system is used in written English now, but you can still use a.m. for the morning, and p.m. for the time after lunch.

6 Vocabulary Exercises

Answer these questions:

a) What day is today? Which date is today? When is your birthday? What did you do the day before yesterday? Which public holidays do you know?

b) Can you tell the days of the week? Can you tell the months of the year backwards?

c) Fill in the gaps in this text:

Emma is really excited about her interview. It will be ________________ the following Wednesday. Today is Monday, which means the interview will be ________________________ .
Emma is glad that the appointment is ________________ one o'clock, as she does not like to risk being late. She usually is ________________ of an hour (15 min) early for important things.
The week ________________ her mum gave her nice clothes for her birthday, which she can wear for the interview. But she has difficulties choosing which shoes to wear – that is always a problem ________________ fall, when you never know what the weather will be like. In the end, she decides to choose shoes ________________ the morning.

355614

C. The Job Interview

The following Wednesday, Emma goes to Munich to Blum Music. Apart from Ms Williams, the HR manager, there is also Emma's (possible) new boss, Mr Blum, present. They ask her some questions about herself, which career she would like to have, why she is interested in this job and then give her an opportunity for her own questions. Within 45 minutes, the job interview is over and Emma is quite happy: she has a good feeling about the interview and the company.

7 Watch the "Dos and Don'ts in job interviews" on YouTube, for example here: http://www.youtube.com/watch?v=S1ucmfPOBV8 and note down the most important rules.

Dos:	Don'ts:
Dress for Success	Don't go off-topic

There are typical questions for job interviews.
Why not find answers for them? – Questionnaire:

- What do you think your strengths are?
- And your weaknesses?
- What do like about this company?
- Why are you interested in this job?

Attention!
Do not answer too personally. Being funny, for instance, is mostly not a strength that is required in a job. Weaknesses should be things that you can change, something you still need to learn or improve, for example a special computer skill.

Questions you might ask are:
What exactly will my responsibilities be? – Is there room for development in this company? Are there many in-house promotions? – Which fringe benefits do I get? – What is my salary?

Vocabulary

appointment	Termin, Verabredung
to appreciate	zu schätzen wissen
to be supposed to	sollen
directions	Wegbeschreibung
enclose	beifügen
employee	Angestellter
employer	Arbeitgeber
fringe benefit	(vertragliche) Nebenleistung
Independence Day	Unabhängigkeitstag
in-house	intern
Labour Day	Tag der Arbeit
opportunity	Gelegenheit
preferences	Vorlieben
public holiday	Feiertag
salary	Einkommen
sociable	umgänglich
Whitsun (UK) / Pentecost (US)	Pfingsten

8 Employment & Companies

Across:

2 – the money someone gets at each end of the month (noun)
5 – the department in a company which buys things (noun)
9 – a person working for a company (noun)
10 – something that is asked or necessary for a position (noun)
11 – the department in a company that takes care of keeping things working (noun)
15 – synonym for open and communicative (adjective)
16 – another word for job or profession (noun)
17 – synonym for possibility (noun)

Down:

1 – having to do with office work, paperwork and regulations (adjective)
3 – a date that someone sets (noun)
4 – to try to get a job (verb)
6 – an ability that you can learn and train (noun)
7 – two or three years in which students learn a job at a company and visit vocational school (noun)
8 – only a short while ago (adverb)
12 – a period of time in which someone can find out if they like a company or a job (noun)
13 – to add something to a letter (verb)
14 – knowing how to do something (adjective)

Possible Answers:

administrative, apply, appointment, apprenticeship, employee, enclose, internship, literate, maintenance, occupation, opportunity, purchase, recently, requirement, salary, skill, sociable

9 **Internet Search:** Find a global player, a company you are interested in and find out as much as possible on the Internet.

On Friday, Emma gets the call that she has the job and can start at the first of the following month!

Starting the Job

In this unit, you will learn:

- How to find your way around an office in English
- How to describe people
- How to do small talk
- Telephone phrases
- To construct and use the passive, the past and future tenses, and the present perfect

A. Around the Office

It is Emma's first day at the office. She is picked up at the reception by her co-worker, John Miller. On their way to her workplace he explains to her that her only task in the first few days is to get accustomed to everything and everybody. As soon as she knows her way around she will be on telephone duty and will then gradually be given some more responsibilities. Emma is excited to hear this and is looking forward to meeting her new colleagues.

1 This is Emma's workplace. Label the various items and facilities.

Attention!
Die deutschen Wörter „Schrank" und „Regal" sind im Englischen nicht einfach zu übersetzen. Während das Deutsche einfach mit näher bezeichnenden Wörtern ein Kompositium bildet, also Akten-schrank, Kleider-schrank, Bücher-regal, stehen im Englischen viele verschiedene Begriffe, z. B. filing cabinet, wardrobe, bookcase.

The Passive Voice

Das Passiv verwendet man dann, wenn nicht klar oder nicht wichtig ist, wer etwas macht, sondern das Objekt betont werden soll. Deshalb wird das Objekt des aktiven Satzes zum Subjekt des passiven Satzes, z. B.

Employees in the sales department sell the products.
→ The products are sold by the employees in the sales department.

Der „Agent“ wird mit „by“ angeschlossen, und kann dann weggelassen werden, wenn keine zusätzliche Aussage verloren geht, z. B.

Somebody has stolen my bike.
→ My bike has been stolen.

Wenn es zwei Objekte gibt, wird das zum neuen Subjekt, das sonst ein indirektes Objekt wäre (also das mit einer Präposition), z. B.

The company offered me a new job.
→ I was offered a new job by the company.
Nicht: A new job was offered **to me** by the company.
Gebildet wird das Passiv immer mit der entsprechenden Form von „to be“ (siehe Anhang S. 109) und dem Past Participle. Das Past Participle bekommt bei regelmäßigen Verben einfach die Endung -ed. Unregelmäßige Verben müssen auswendig gelernt werden. Das Past Participle ist hier die dritte Form.

Attention!
Im Englischen steht am Anfang immer das Subjektpronomen, nicht wie im Deutschen manchmal das Objektpronomen. Vgl.: Mir wurde ein Job angeboten (siehe Anhang S. 111).

2 **Grammar Exercise:** Form passive sentences. Omit the agent if possible.

1. Human resources employ new staff.

____

2. Workers mount our products in the production.

____

3. Somebody makes coffee in the morning.

____

4. Logistics organise the transport of our products.

____

5. John gave Emma a little welcome present for her first day at work.

____

Idea:
Open your bag and take out one random thing. Go on the Internet and try to find out how it is produced. Then try to explain it. You will need the passive voice to do this.

Grammar

3 John then tells her about the different departments. Match the words (1-10) with their description a-j.

1. human resources
2. accounting
3. sales
4. purchase department
5. logistics
6. administration
7. production
8. health and safety
9. quality department
10. environment and energy

a The products of a company are sold here.
b This department takes care of everything that is organised, documented and filed.
c Things are built, produced or made here.
d Invoices are written here and the finances are dealt with.
e This department ensures that every staff stays well and healthy.
f Staff in this department deals with complaints and is responsible for good products.
g This department takes care of employing new staff and organising people.
h All the necessary things for production and work are bought here.
i People here make sure that energy consumption is reduced and regulations to protect the environment are complied to.
j Transports are organised in this department.

Since Blum Music is a very small company, many departments have only one or two employees. Only the production has **supervisors,** the rest of the company has a very flat hierarchy and most people **answer** directly **to** the boss, Carl Blum.

Vocabulary

accustomed	gewohnt
to answer to	jmd. Rechenschaft ablegen, hier: jmd. untergeben sein.
ballpoint pen	Kugelschreiber
coffee maker	Kaffemaschine
complaint	Beschwerde
to comply to (regulations)	einhalten (Regeln)
copying machine	Kopierer
desk	Schreibtisch
energy consumption	Energieverbrauch
to ensure, to make sure	sicherstellen
file	Akte
to file	ablegen
folder	Ordner
headset	Kopfhörer mit Sprechfunktion
hole puncher	Locher
invoice	Rechnung
mouse	Maus
mousepad	Mauspad
printer	Drucker
scanner	Scanner
sort pocket	Ablagefach
staff	Mitarbeiter
stapler	Tacker
supervisor	Vorgesetzer, Vorarbeiter

Attention!
Die Bildung der Vergangenheit ist für Deutsche besonders schwierig. Wir benutzen mündlich fast nur das Perfekt, und das Imperfekt in der Schriftsprache. Die Regeln im Englischen sind sehr klar, und ganz anders. Auf gar keinen Fall darf man die Zeit einfach mitübersetzen. Man muss immer das Wort in der Grundform übersetzen, und dann überlegen, welche Zeit im Englischen steht.

The past tenses

The Past Simple

Das Past Simple wird bei regelmäßigen Verben mit der Endung -ed gebildet, z. B. call > called, und sehen genauso aus wie das Past Participle, das man zur Bildung der Perfect Tenses und des Passivs verwendet. Unregelmäßige Verben (siehe Anhang) müssen auswendig gelernt werden, z. B. go > went. Diese Form steht nie in Kombination mit einem anderen Verbteil. In Fragen und Sätzen mit „not" wird „did" ergänzt, und im Anschluss steht die Grundform, z. B. I didn't call. He didn't go. Did you call? Did he go?

Das Past Simple beschreibt die abgeschlossene Vergangenheit, steht also mit konkreten Zeitangaben.

The Past Progressive

Das Past Progressive (Continuous) wird mit der Past Simple Form von „to be" und dem Verb in der -ing Form gebildet.

Person	Singular	Plural
1. Ps	I was going	we were going
2. Ps	you were going	you were going
3. Ps	he was going she was going it was going	they were going

Das Past Progressive verwendet man, um Gleichzeitigkeit auszudrücken. Es steht also entweder mit einer Handlung im Past Simple, die in den Handlungszeitraum fällt, oder mit einer genauen Zeitangabe. Das Past Progressive wird auch „Alibizeit" genannt, z. B.

What were you doing when your husband was murdered?
At two p.m. I was sleeping.

The Past Perfect

Das Past Perfect wird mit „had" und dem Past Participle gebildet. Bei regelmäßigen Verben wird das Past Participle genau wie das Past Simple mit der Endung -ed gebildet, z. B. I had called. Die unregelmäßigen Verben müssen gelernt werden, z. B. He had gone.

Das Past Perfect verwendet man, um Vorzeitigkeit auszudrücken. Es steht also nur dann, wenn bereits etwas in der Vergangenheit erzählt wird, und man dann noch weiter zurückblicken will. Diese Zeit ist deckungsgleich mit dem deutschen Plusquamperfekt. Auch hier gibt es eine Progressive Form (had been going), die verwendet wird, wenn etwas bis zu dem Zeitpunkt andauert, von dem man spricht, z. B.

When I arrived at the party, Tom had already left. (Tom ist also schon gegangen, Vorzeitigkeit.)

When I arrived at the party, people had been dancing for hours. (Sie tanzten schon lange, und tanzten noch.)

4 **Grammar Exercise:** Past simple, progressive or perfect? Fill in the right form of the verbs.

When Emma ____________________ (get) the job at Music Blum, she ____________________ (must) move to Munich. She ____________________ (already, save) some money to buy new furniture and pay for the move, but she ____________________ (not expect) that it would be so hard to find a flat in Munich. She ____________________ (search) on the Internet, ____________________ (read) the local newspapers and finally ____________________ (call) some real estate agencies. She ____________________ (be) quite desperate, when her mum ____________________ (have) an idea. She ____________________ (contact) an old friend, whose daughter Rebecca also studies in Munich. Fortunately, Rebecca ____________________ (search) for a new flat mate anyway, and ____________________ (offer) the room to Emma.

Two days later, Emma ____________________ (move). They ____________________ (rent) a transporter, which her dad would drive. She ____________________ (pack) many boxes. While they ____________________ (load) them into the transporter, one of them ____________________ (break) open. Emma ____________________ (look) guiltily at the many books on the street – she ____________________ (put) to many heavy things into the box. Her dad simply ____________________ (laugh) and ____________________ (use) some package tape to stick it back together.

Emma ____________________ (be) very tired, as she ____________________ (can, not) sleep the night before. So she ____________________ (sleep) most of the time on the long way to Munich. Her dad only ____________________ (wake) her up to have lunch and shortly before they ____________________ (arrive) in Munich.

When they ____________________ (arrive) at the flat, Rebecca and her other flat mate, Sandra, ____________________ (wait). They ____________________ (help) carry Emma's things into her room. The bed and the wardrobe Emma ____________________ (order) on the Internet, ____________________ (arrive) the day before. Emma ____________________ (mount) the wardrobe with her dad, while Rebecca and Sandra ____________________ (put) the bed together.

Three hours later everything ____________________ (be) unpacked and Emma's dad ____________________ (invite) her and her new flat mates out to dinner. Her dad ____________________ (spend) the night in a nearby hotel. He ____________________ (fly) back to Hamburg the next morning and ____________________ (leave) the transporter at the airport. When Emma ____________________ (say) her goodbyes and ____________________ (go) back to her apartment alone on the subway, she ____________________ (feel) really grown up for the first time in her life.

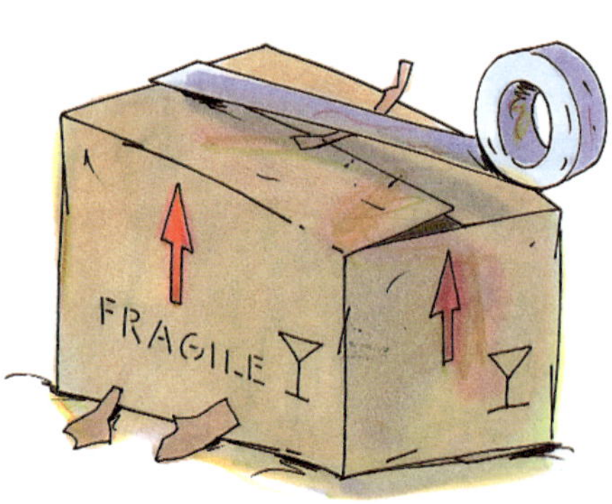

B. Meeting Colleagues

After Emma has seen her workplace and put her bag there, John introduces her to the other colleagues in the office. There is Katherine, a tall blond woman in her mid-twenties; then there is George, a middle-aged man with brown hair and a very friendly smile; and Patrick, a young guy with short, blond hair and a very sporty look.

5 Bring the conversation into the right order.

1. **Patrick:** “I'm Patrick. Nice to meet you.”
2. **Emma:** “Yes, I have an appointment with our boss in a few minutes. Speak to you later.”
3. **Patrick:** “Hi, how are you?”
4. **Emma:** “Thanks, I will.”
5. **Patrick:** “My tasks mainly involve dealing with customers. You are here to support our team, yes?”
6. **Emma:** “Fine. Hi, I'm Emma.”
7. **Patrick:** “Oh, and we usually all have lunch together. Do you want to join us?”
8. **Emma:** “Nice to meet you, too. What are your responsibilities here?”
9. **Patrick:** “Great. Then I'll leave you to your work.”
10. **Emma:** “Yes, I hope I'll be of some help soon.”
11. **Emma:** “Yes, I would love to. Thanks.”
12. **Patrick:** “I'm sure you will. Have a good first day. And if you have any questions, just ask.”

At lunch, Emma gets to know her colleagues a little bit more. John is a very energetic man, he has been with the company the longest. He optimises processes as a part of continuous improvement and has many long-term projects concerning energy, safety or quality. Katherine is very cheerful and tells Emma about the best places to go out. She deals with orders and is the administrative link to the production. George is a family man, very laid-back and sociable. He is responsible for the production and quality. Patrick confirms Emma's first impression, when he tells them about the bike tour he did in the Alps the weekend before. He is quite handsome and very talkative.

6 Which other words to describe people's personality do you know? Try to describe three people you know, and look up the words you don't know in a dictionary.

Vocabulary

to be responsible for	verantwortlich sein für
cheerful	fröhlich
concerning	betreffend
to confirm	bestätigen
continuous improvement – also: lean management or Kaizen	kontinuierlicher Verbesserungs-prozess
energetic	energiegeladen
handsome	gutaussehend
impression	Eindruck
to involve	miteinbeziehen, hier: beinhalten
laid-back	entspannt
link	Verbindung
responsibility	Verantwortung, Verantwartungs-bereich
sociable	kontaktfreudig, gesellig
to support	unterstützen
talkative	gesprächig, redselig
task	Aufgabe

Small Talk – Showing Interest

It is natural to show interest in a conversation by making sounds like "mhm", "yeah", or "uhuh". But to keep up the conversation you will want to say more. There are some words or phrases that you can say as a confirmation or to show interest, such as "I see.", "Exactly.", or "Really?". You can also echo words or phrases, for example
I went to Paris over the weekend. → "Did you?" or "Paris?".

Of course, to have a good conversation, you should ask real questions. There are closed questions (to be answered with "Yes" or "No") or open questions. Every question that starts with a question word is automatically an open question. Ideally, you should not only ask questions, but also tell something that is related to what the other person has said.

7 Match the strategies given in the box with the reaction to the statement:

"I went to the movies last weekend."

1. I like movies. ______________________
2. Mhm. ______________________
3. Really? ______________________
4. Did you? ______________________
5. Which movie did you see? ______________________
6. To the movies? ______________________
7. Did you like the film? ______________________

echo question	*open question*	*sound*	*standard phrase*
word	*closed question*	*echo*	*personal statement*

8 **The small talk game.** Choose one of the following topics and speak for at least one minute about it. Your partner's task is to keep up the conversation after your initial statement. Try to keep up the conversation as long as possible, but at least for five minutes.

- movies
- music
- holidays
- family and friends
- TV

- sports
- leisure time
- job
- news
- animals and pets

Idea:
Emma is a big fan of all kinds of music. One of her favourite songs is "Both Sides Now" by Joni Mitchell, because the lyrics are so interesting. Translate the lyrics of your favourite song.

355624

The Present Perfect

Das Present Perfect wird mit „have“ gebildet, bei der 3. Person Singular steht „has“, und dem Past Participle, also dem Verb mit der Endung -ed oder der 3. Form der unregelmäßigen Verben.

Wie der Name sagt, hat das Present Perfect einen Bezug zur Gegenwart. Es beschreibt zum einen Handlungen und Vorgänge, die in der Vergangenheit begonnen haben und noch andauern. Diese Aussagen stehen auch gerne im Present Perfect Progressive (Continuous), z. B. I have been working here since 2002.

Zum anderen werden mit dem Present Perfect Vorgänge beschrieben, die einen Bezug zur oder eine Konsequenz für die Gegenwart haben, vergleiche:

> Attention!
> Das Present Perfect ist für Deutsche besonders schwierig, da es bei uns keine Zeit gibt, die wir genauso verwenden. Im Deutschen steht entweder das Präsens, z. B. „Ich arbeite hier seit 2002.“ oder es macht nur einen Unterschied im Sprachregister, ob das Imperfekt oder Perfekt steht, z. B. „Er brach sich seinen Arm.“, „Er hat sich seinen Arm gebrochen.“ Im Englischen gibt es klare Regeln, wann das Past Simple steht und wann das Present Perfect.

Tom broke his arm on Saturday. → past simple; Zeitangabe und das Ereignis selbst steht im Vordergrund.

Tom has broken his arm, so he cannot play the next game. → present perfect; wichtig ist, dass er den Arm noch gebrochen hat und er nicht spielen kann.

9 Fill in the right form of the verb: past simple or present perfect.

Now that she ____________________ (move) to Munich, Emma wants to find a new band or opportunity to make music. She ____________________ (play) the guitar since she was eight. For the last three years she ____________________ (be) the lead guitarist in a band called “Afterthought”, but she had to leave them, of course. The band ____________________ (record) a demo a year ago, but nothing big ever ____________________ (happen). Now she wants to join a less ambitious band who simply wants to play the occasional gig. So Emma ____________________ (decided) to put a flyer up in some local music store, and one week after she ____________________ (do) this, Frankie calls her. He tells Emma that they ____________________ (search) for a new guitarist, and invites her for a jam session. The session goes really well, Frankie is impressed that Emma ____________________ (play) the guitar for so long. They decide to give it a try.

Exercises: the question form

10 Fill in the missing part of the tense, the right forms of “to be”, “have” or “do”.

These are parts of the conversation Emma had with Frankie.

1. ____________________ you hear that? That was awesome.
2. How long ____________________ you been playing the guitar? For five years.
3. What song ____________________ we playing? “Run”, a modern classic.
4. ____________________ you rehearse regularly? Yes, every second Monday.

11 **The “Who am I?”-game.** Sit in a circle of a maximum of five people. Your right neighbour counter-clockwise writes a name of a famous person on a paper. You should do the same for your left neighbour. Then, clockwise, you are allowed to ask closed questions in order to find out whose name is on the paper. You can ask as long as you get “Yes” or “I don’t know” as an answer. Once you get a “No” it is your neighbour’s turn. The game ends when everyone has guessed who the famous people are.

C. Telephone Duty

In her first days at work, Emma has met almost everyone who works for Music Blum, and has learned what they are responsible for. She has been shown the filing system and internal documentation. Most orders are handled in a software program that was customised for the company. Besides dealing with the mail, organising meetings and entering incoming orders into the system, it is Emma's task to answer the phone calls that come in over the central line.

Here are some standard phrases for answering the phone:

Answering the phone:

This is Emma Frey. This is Emma Frey speaking.
Music Blum. My name is Emma Frey.
How can I help you? What can I do for you?

The caller wants to speak to a colleague:

Just a moment please. I'll put you through.
I'm afraid the line is busy. Would you like to leave a message?
Unfortunately, Mr Smith / Ms Smith is out of the office today. Can he / she call you back tomorrow?

Getting the caller's ID:

Would you like to leave your contact details?
Could you spell your name, please?
And your email address was?
Let me read that back to you.

Getting information:

I'm calling to ask about ...
I was wondering if it is possible to ...
I'm afraid I didn't get that. Could you repeat it please?
I was just calling to confirm the appointment on the 6th.

Attention!
Women are now addressed with a neutral Ms (spoken with a long i). Miss is completely outdated, and Mrs is only used with women in the context of marriage, or if they insist on it.

Idea:
Go on the Internet and learn the English alphabet with an ABC Song, such as the "Alphabet Rap" on YouTube. Then pick up a dictionary and spell difficult words to a partner. Check if he or she wrote the words correctly and tell them what they mean.

Vocabulary

ambitious	ehrgeizig
busy	beschäftigt, hier: besetzt
clockwise	im Uhrzeigersinn
confirmation	Bestätigung
counterclockwise	gegen den Uhrzeigersinn
customised	auf den Kunden zugeschnitten
to enter	eingeben
impressed	beeindruckt
incoming	herein kommend
initial	beginnend
occasional	gelegentlich
opportunity	Gelgenheit, Möglichkeit
to read back	wiederholen

355626

12 Emma's busy day on the phone. Fill in the missing words given in the box in the following telephone conversations.

Emma: *Blum Music. My name is Emma Frey. How can I help you?*

Caller 1: *Hello. This is Megan Porter from Top Tabs. I would like to ________________ (1) a meeting with your purchase department.*
Emma: *Good morning Ms. Porter. May I ________________ (2) what this is about?*
Caller 1: *Yes, certainly. I would like to present our new product range of publications, particularly our books with lyrics and chords. I could imagine a ________________ (3) would be a good idea.*
Emma: *Thank you very much. If you'd be so kind as to leave your ________________ (4) details, then I'll ________________ (5) on the information, and someone from the purchase department will get back to you as soon as possible.*
Caller 1: *Sure, my number is ... .*

Caller 2: *Yes, is this Blum Music? The guitar company?*
Emma: *Yes, you've called the right number. What can I do for you?*
Caller 2: *Well, I'm ________________ (6) because I bought one of your guitars and I'm really not happy with it.*
Emma: *I'm sorry to hear that. If it's okay ________________ (7) you, I will put you right through to customer ________________ (8).*
Caller 2: *Yes, please.*
Emma: *Ok. Have a good day.*

Caller 3: *Good afternoon, this is Taylor Brown. May I speak to Patrick, please?*
Emma: *Good afternoon. I'm ________________ (9) Patrick is out of ________________ (10) for the afternoon. Would you like to leave a message?*
Caller 3: *Hm. That's not good. Could you please ask Patrick to call me ________________ (11) as soon as possible. I'm afraid it is rather ________________ (12).*
Emma: *Of course. I will also try him on his cell. Does he have your number?*
Caller 3: *Yes. That'd be great.*
Emma: *All right. If I don't ________________ (13) him this afternoon, I will make sure he calls you first thing tomorrow morning.*
Caller 3: *Perfect. Thanks.*
Emma: *Not at all.*

Caller 4: *Hi, this is - - -*
Emma: *Pardon. I didn't get that. Could you repeat please?*
Caller 4: *Ah, cell phone ________________ (14) is really bad here. My name is Nikhil Dasgupta. I would like to inform you about a delay in our delivery.*
Emma: *Okay. That's not very good news. Could you tell me our order number please?*
Caller 4: *Of course. It's 039403-12.*
Emma: *And what seems to be the problem with the ________________ (15)?*
Caller 4: *Well, unfortunately bad weather ________________ (16) have delayed the transport.*
Emma: *Could you tell me when we can expect the delivery?*
Caller 4: *I cannot be sure, but I think it should arrive three days after the original delivery ________________ (17).*
Emma: *Okay, I will enter it into our system, and the purchase department will probably get back to you with ________________ (18) details. ...*

set up – date – further – contact – calling – inquire – cooperation – pass – office – complaints – with – urgent – reach – reception – delivery – conditions – afraid – back

Role Play

13 Sit back to back with a partner. Go to the partner files on page 113 and 116 respectively, and role play the telephone conversations.

355627

The Future Tenses

Present progressive

Das Present Progressive (Bildung siehe Seite 9) wird für feststehende persönliche Pläne verwendet, z. B.
I am going to a party on Saturday.

Attention!
Im Deutschen drücken wir vieles in der Gegenwart aus, das eigentlich in der Zukunft liegt. Das ist im Englischen auch so, nur dass hier das Present Progressive verwendet wird. Die Will-Future benützen Deutsche viel zu häufig, da sie genauso wie die „werden"-Zukunft gebildet wird.

Going-to-Future

Die Going-to-Future bildet man indem man die entsprechende Form von „to be" im Present Simple verwendet (siehe Seite 7), und daran going to und das Verb im Infinitiv anhängt.

Für die Going-to-Future entscheidet sich der Sprecher, wenn er persönliche Pläne ausdrückt, die aber noch nicht sicher sind. In diesem Sinne „vorhaben etwas zu tun" gibt es auch ein „was / were going to do sth.", das einen vergangenen Plan ausdrückt, z. B.
I am going to become a rockstar when I grow up.
I was going to tell you, but then I forgot.

Zum anderen entscheidet sich der Sprecher für die Going-to-Future, wenn er Vorraussagen trifft, die auf gerade gemachten Erfahrungen und Wahrnehmungen beruhen, z. B.
Look at the clouds. It's going to rain soon.

Will-Future

Die Will-Future bildet man mit dem Modalverb „will" und dem Infinitiv. Sie wird im persönlichen Bereich nur bei spontanen Entscheidungen, Versprechen und Forderungen verwendet, z. B.
I'll have a coke, please.
You will come and pick me up, yes?!

Sonst beschreibt sie faktische Vorraussagen und Dinge die personenunabhängig in der Zukunft liegen, z. B.
I expect he will be here soon.
Man will live on Mars one day.

Bei Zeitplänen, Fahrplänen oder Tagesordnungen steht das **Present Simple.** Außer hierfür und im Conditional Typ 1 wird das Present Simple nicht für die Zukunft verwendet.

Advanced Future Tenses

Will-Future Progressive

Das Will-Future Progressive wird mit „will be" und dem Verb in der -ing Form gebildet. Es steht, wenn man beschreiben will, dass in der Zukunft ein Vorgang gerade passieren wird, z. B.
Tomorrow at this time, I will be travelling home.

Future Perfect

Das Future Perfect wird mit „will have" und dem Verb im Past Participle gebildet. Es steht, wenn man beschreiben will, dass in der Zukunft ein Vorgang beendet sein wird, z. B.
Tomorrow at this time, I will have finished this book.

Auch hier gibt es ein Progressive, das mit „will have been" und dem Verb in der -ing Form gebildet wird. Es beschreibt einen Vorgang, der in der Zukunft schon eine Weile angedauert hat, und noch andauert, z. B.
Tomorrow at this time, I will have been travelling for three hours.

355628

14 Fill in the correct form of the verb: present progressive, going-to-future, will-future. In some spaces you will simply have to put in the right modal.

At lunch, Emma chats with Katherine about some plans she has been making.

Emma: Now that I live here, I ______________________ (explore) Bavaria in more detail.

Katherine: You should. What ______________________ (you, do) first?

Emma: Well, next weekend I ______________________ (hike) in the Alps, before it ______________________ (get) to cold.

Katherine: Great. With whom ______________________ (you, go)?

Emma: With Frankie, my band mate. I think he ______________________ (take) good care of me. I'm not a very experienced hiker.

Katherine: Do you have good shoes?

Emma: I ______________________ (buy) some this afternoon.

Katherine: Okay, but promise that you ______________________ (wear) them tomorrow and on Friday to break them in.

Emma: I ______________________ , I promise. Do you have any other suggestions?

Katherine: About shoes? Or Frankie? Just kidding. People always tell you about beer and the Oktoberfest, but here in Munich there is a lot of history. ______________________ (do) a guided tour?

Emma: I hadn't thought about that, yet. But of course I ______________________ . ______________________ (you, join) me?

Katherine: Why not. It's been ages since I did it. I think this ______________________ (be) a lot of fun.

Emma: Great. You should know something about the place you live at, shouldn't you?

Katherine: Absolutely. And Emma, I ______________________ (take) you out the next free weekend and show you some places to hang out.

Emma: That sounds really fabulous. Shall we order?

Katherine: Yes, I'm really hungry. I ______________________ (have) a huge portion of pasta.

Emma: You are full of great ideas today.

Idea:
Watch your favourite movie in English. If you have problems understanding the language, turn on the English subtitles.

Vocabulary

to set up	einrichten, festsetzen
to inquire	fragen, nachfragen
publication	Veröffentlichung
lyrics	Liedtext
particularly	besonders
I'm afraid	Ich befürchte
cell (phone), mobile phone	Handy
delay	Verspätung
delivery	Lieferung
far, further, furthest	weit, weiter(e), am weitesten
reception	Empfang
urgent	dringend
condition(s)	Bedingung(en)
to break sth. in	(Schuhe) einlaufen, (Kleidung) eintragen, etc
suggestion	Vorschlag
to hike	wandern
just kidding	Nur Spaß
to hang out	Zeit verbringen

15 Office work

Across:

2 – to stick to regulations
3 – in relation to, referring
6 – if someone tells you about a possible way to do something, they are making a ...
8 – something to file print-outs in
10 – making something better is an ...
11 – a kind of boss
12 – a kind letter sent to people who have to pay a certain amount of money for something they have bought
13 – something that is assigned to you, you have to do it
14 – beginning with
15 – something or someone does not arrive on time
16 – a possibility to do something

Down:

1 – if somebody is speaking on the phone, their line is ...
2 – the state that something is in
3 – if something is wrong with a product, customers will file this
4 – if you have to take care of something, it is your ...
5 – to make sure something is correct
7 – if something is done according to a customer's specification
9 – a product arrives at a certain place

16 **Tell Us – a board game.** Play the game on the next page. It is a normal board game where you roll a dice and move the according amount of spaces. Every space contains a piece of information you should "tell us" about. Speak for at least a minute. Your counterclockwise neighbor should then ask a follow-up question referring to what you have said. Watch the tenses while you are talking!

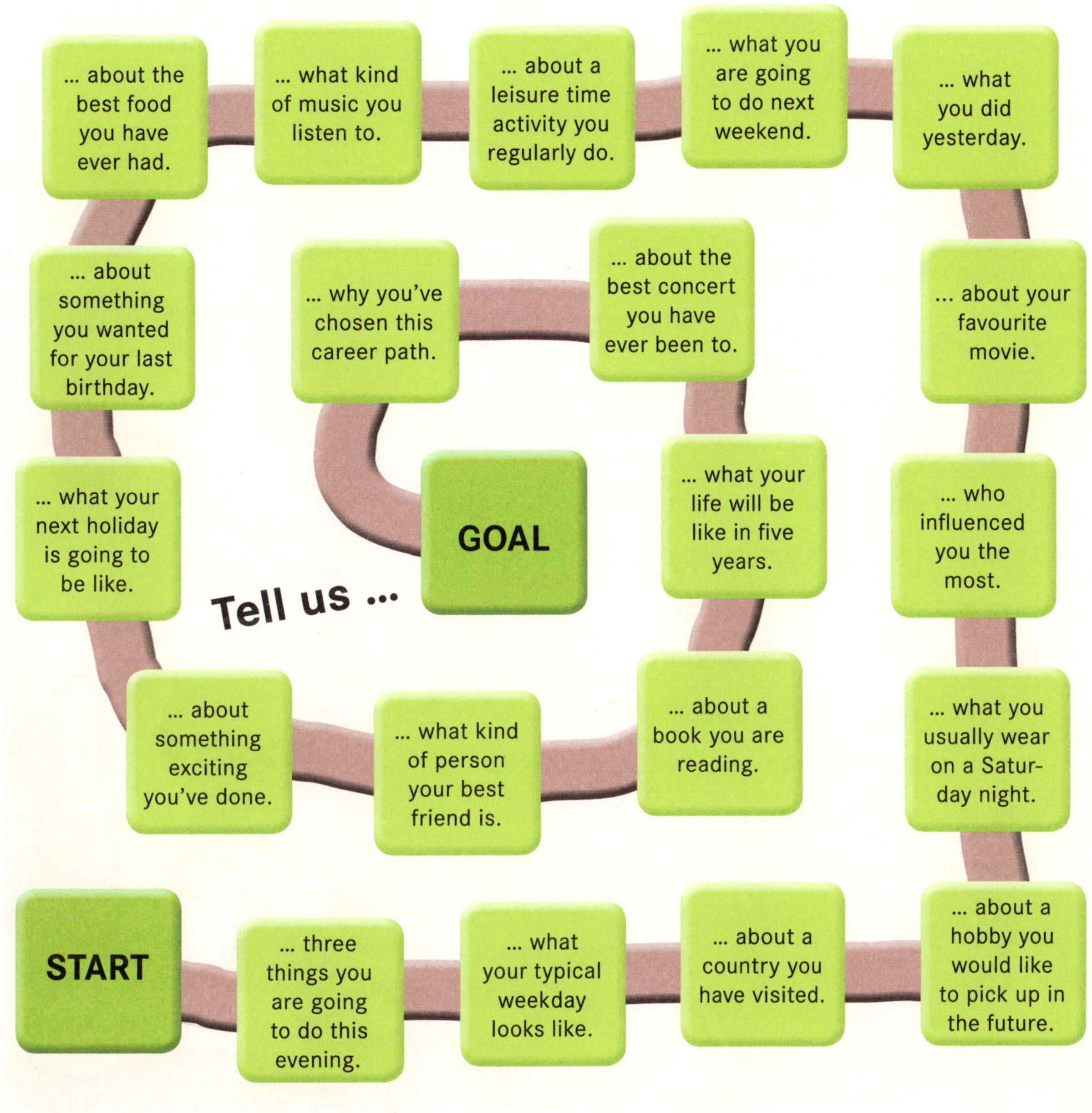
Tell us …
START
… three things you are going to do this evening.
… what your typical weekday looks like.
… about a country you have visited.
… about a hobby you would like to pick up in the future.
… what you usually wear on a Satur-day night.
… who influenced you the most.
… about your favourite movie.
… what you did yesterday.
… what you are going to do next weekend.
… about a leisure time activity you regularly do.
… what kind of music you listen to.
… about the best food you have ever had.
… about something you wanted for your last birthday.
… what your next holiday is going to be like.
… about something exciting you've done.
… what kind of person your best friend is.
… about a book you are reading.
… what your life will be like in five years.
… about the best concert you have ever been to.
… why you've chosen this career path.
GOAL

In this unit, you will learn:

- How to welcome visitors
- How to make small talk
- How to write a memo
- Standard phrases for emails and letters
- How to place orders and make offers
- How to deal with customer complaints
- Basic logistics and stock control
- The language of sales and purchases
- The difference between adjectives and adverbs
- How to compare adjectives
- About modal auxiliaries

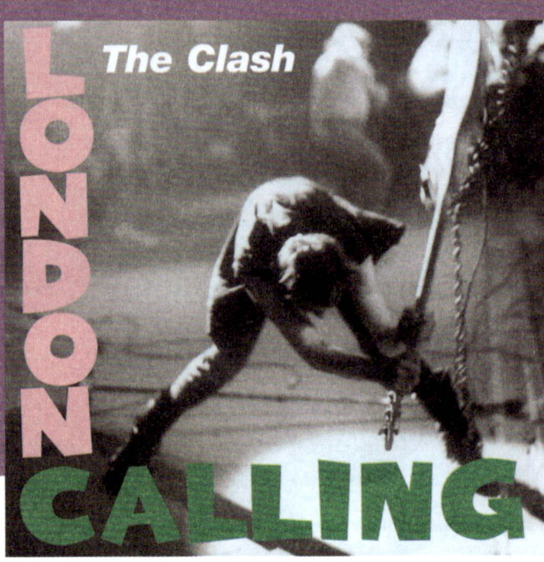

355632

A. Daily Business

After a week at Blum, Emma already knows her way around the office. She gets her first assignment, which is to assist Nadine Summers, who is responsible for fan articles. The British customer Eventline has so far only ordered posters, but has indicated that they would like to expand their order to T-shirts and other fan articles if negotiations go well. A meeting has been arranged and it is Emma's responsibility to receive the customer, Mr Jackson, and later to take the minutes.

1 Insert the words in the boxes to find phrases that are helpful in social interactions like these.

meet – refreshments – beverages – will – accommodation – would – let – great – do – trip – happy – for – help – take care

Emma: Good morning, Mr Jackson. Welcome to Blum Music. My name is Emma Frey and I will ____________ you find everything here today and ____________ of anything you might need.

Mr Jackson: Hello Ms Frey. Nice to ____________ you. Where do we go first?

Emma: First, we will pick up your ID at the reception. (*They go to the reception and pick up the ID*). How was your ____________ ?

Mr Jackson: It was fine, thank you.

Emma: And your ____________ is alright, too?

Mr Jackson: Yes, I checked into the hotel late last night, but the hotel staff was very attentive.

Emma: I am ____________ to hear that. Okay, now that we've got your ID, ____________ me take you to the meeting room. (*Once they've arrived there*) ____________ you like any ____________ ? Something to drink maybe, we can offer some cold or hot ____________ .

Mr Jackson: I had a large breakfast, but some coffee and water would be ____________ .

Emma: Okay, I ____________ be back in a minute. ____________ you need anything else?

Mr Jackson: I believe that is all ____________ now. Thank you.

> **Attention! Small Talk**
> Making small talk is often underestimated in Business English. Yet think about it: how often do you start a conversation with a stranger by talking about the weather or something that is happening in your country? In business, you will need small talk while you are walking to a room, having lunch or dinner, or during a coffee break. Be open for many topics and listen carefully to find out what your business partner is interested in.

Role Play

2 How to welcome guests

In turns, be Emma and Mr Jackson, and role play Mr Jackson's arrival at Blum Music. The stages should include: welcome, small talk, going to the meeting room, offering refreshments. You can and should vary the phrases you use. For more ideas go to page 118.

3 Ask one question to open a conversation on each of the following topics.

Make sure it is an open question (starting with a question word). Then try to have a conversation with a partner about this topic or something else as long as possible, but at least for 3 minutes.
Try to imagine your partner is a business partner and you do not want to get too personal!

weather

sports

current events

holidays

food

popular culture

hobbies

family

The meeting goes well and the negotiation is successful. Emma's task now is to type up a report from the minutes. She then sends it to her department and Mr Jackson.

Meeting Eventline

Posters – usual conditions – 10 Cent per piece, 8 Cent per piece when order is more than 1,000.

T-Shirts-motives: two or three? two saves cost on both sides
Decision: three, more attractive to fans, but orders in not under 1,000 pieces.
Cost: € 4 per piece, € 3.50 when order more than 3,000.

Other fan articles: Mr Jackson peruses catalogue, would like something more original.
Consent: marketing department should develop new ideas and present possibilities in 3 weeks.

Terms of delivery and payment as with posters.

4 Write Emma's memo for her department and Eventline. Include an opening segment, a summary segment and a closing segment.

To: Martin Jackson (Eventline); Nadine Summers, Carl Blum (Blum Music)
From: Emma Frey
Date: Oct 15th, 201...
Subject: Meeting Eventline

Idea:
If you have a new task at work, the Internet can be an immense help. Go to http://www.wikihow.com/Write-a-Memo or http://esl.about.com/od/businessenglishwriting/a/bizdocs_2.htm to find out more about when and how to write a memo.

Vocabulary: Computer screen and software

5 Fill in the German translations below the English words. Use a dictionary if necessary.

Attention!
Online dictionaries or dictionary apps are becoming more and more popular. If you use them German – English and you do not know the English word you want to use, look it up in a second source, ideally in a printed dictionary that gives you some context.

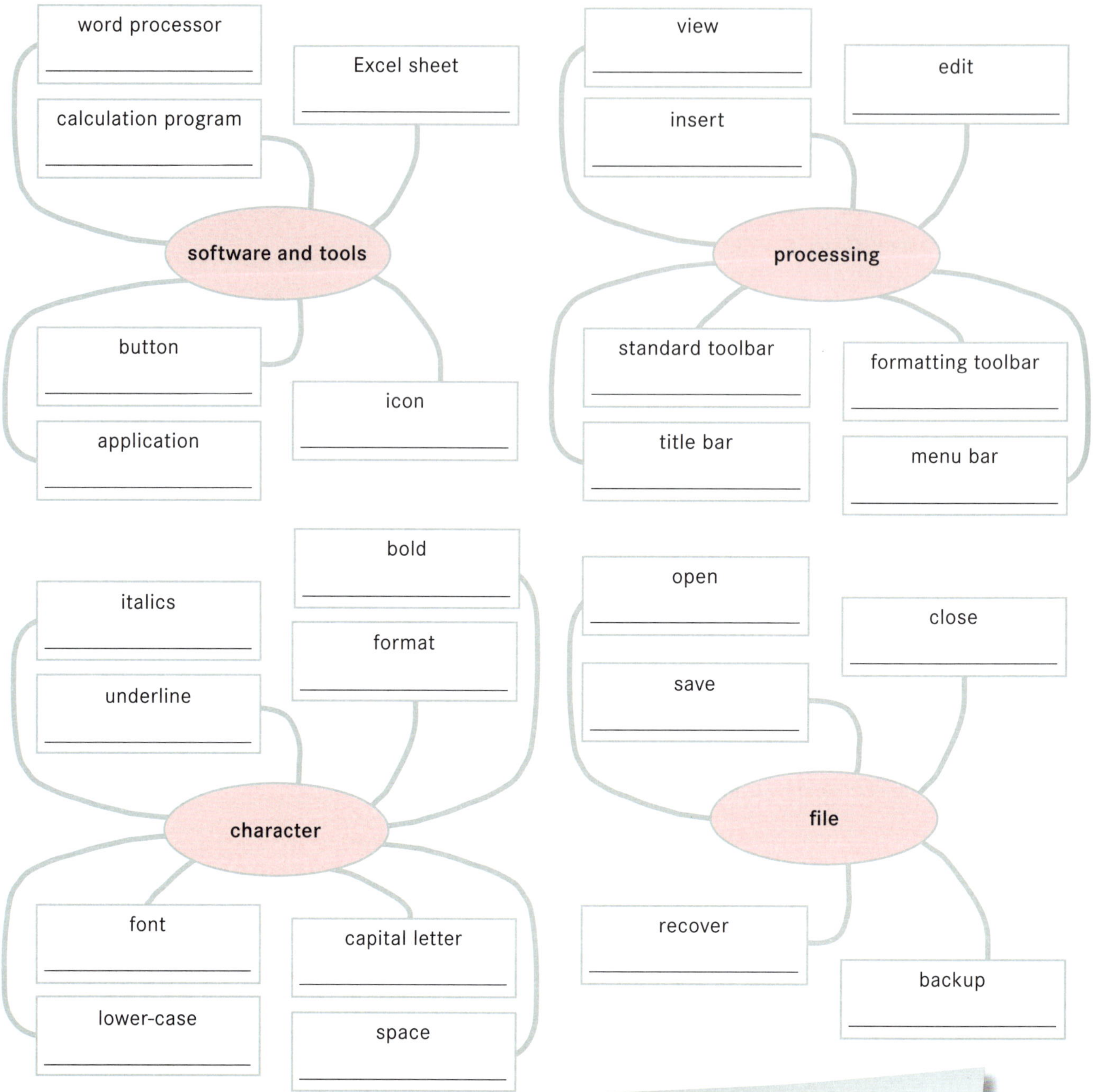

Nadine Schwebling asks Emma to write another memo to the department concerning this year's Christmas party. Here are Emma's notes:

6 Type Emma's second memo on your computer using a word processing program. During the process think about the individual steps and what they are called in English. Note them down below.

355636

Adjectives and Adverbs

Adjektive (Eigenschaftswörter) beschreiben Nomen (Substantive, Hauptwörter) genauer; im Deutschen werden Adjektive an Genus (Geschlecht) und Kasus (Fall) des Nomens angepasst. Im Englischen gibt es das nicht. Adverbien (Umstandswörter) können entweder die Art und Weise beschreiben, wie etwas getan wird, oder sie stehen für Orts- und Zeitangaben. Manchmal beziehen sich Adverbien auch auf einen ganzen Satz, dann werden sie vorangestellt und mit einem Komma vom Hauptsatz abgesetzt.

Adjectives	Adverbs
- describe nouns e.g. This is a beautiful dress. - are used with verbs that actually describe the noun (= link verbs) e.g. Peter is nice. The soup smells good.	- describe verbs e.g. Kate sings beautifully. - describe adjectives e.g. This is really awful. - describe adverbs - refer to a sentence

Meistens bildet man das Adverb einfach, indem ein -ly an ein Adjektiv hängt. Es gibt ein paar unregelmäßige Adverbien und ein paar, die genauso aussehen wie das Adjektiv. Bei einigen kommt es auch auf die Bedeutung an (siehe Anhang, Seite 109).

e.g. good - well.
He is a good driver. He drives well.

hard - hardly
He works hard. = Er arbeitet viel.
He hardly works. = Er arbeitet kaum.

Attention!
Das Adjektiv *well* heißt wohlauf, gesund. "I hope you are well" heißt also, man hofft, der andere sei wohlauf.

7 In the evening Emma takes the subway to get home. She listens to a podcast on her mp3-player. Choose the correct form: adjective or adverb.

Speaker: We are talking today about a wonderful/wonderfully new/newly book by Taketa Darin, who became quite/quitly famous/famously with her last novel *Where the Willows Cry*. Her recent/recently published masterpiece is called *Till the End of Winter* and it is the breathtaking/ breathtakingly account of a family's struggle with Alzheimer's disease. It is beautiful/beautifully written and a real/really page-turner. Here to talk about the book is the author Taketa Darin. (*Pause*). Welcome to our podcast, Taketa.

Taketa: Thanks for having me. I am happy/happily to be here.

Speaker: Taketa, your book has been received absolute/absolutely positive/positively. Did you expect such a warm/warmly reception?

Taketa: I think as an author it is important/importantly not to think about the critics while you are writing. But now I grateful/gratefully enjoy the good/well reviews. Particular/Particularly, because I worked extreme/extremely hard/hardly on this novel.

Speaker: Well, the writing seems effortless/ effortlessly. What was harder than before?

Taketa: The research took a tremendous/ tremendously amount of time. And it was not always nice/nicely to read and hear these stories.

Speaker: Sure. However, it sounds interesting/ interestingly. Why don't you tell us more about your research process?

Taketa: Of course, ...
At that moment, Emma arrives home and decides to listen to the rest of the podcast while ironing her shirts.

Idea:
A podcast is (like) a radio show that you can download from the Internet. There are video podcasts and audio podcasts. For travelling or doing household chores, an audio podcast is a good idea to get informed and to practice your listening skills. Go on the Internet, search for a podcast that interests you and listen to it. If you like it, why don't you subscribe and listen to it on a regular basis?

Vocabulary

accommodation	Unterbringung, Unterkunft
account	hier: Bericht
application	Anwendung
assignment	Aufgabe
to assist	helfen
beverages	Getränke
bold	fett (gedruckt)
breathtaking	atemberaubend
button	Knopf
capital letter	Großbuchstabe
character	Schriftzeichen
condition	Bedingung, Zustand
consent	Abmachung, Übereinkunft
to correspond	korrespondieren, sich schreiben
current	aktuell
disease	Krankheit
effortless	anstrengungslos, unangestrengt
Excel sheet	Excel Tabelle
famous	berühmt
font	Schrift
household chores	Aufgaben im Haushalt
to indicate	andeuten
in turns	abwechselnd
italics	kursiv
lower-case	Kleinbuchstabe
masterpiece	Meisterwerk
minutes	Protokoll
negotiation	Verhandlung
page-turner	spannendes Buch, bei dem man schnell die Seiten umblättert
particular	besonders
to phrase	formulieren
personal	persönlich, privat
quite	ziemlich
to receive	empfangen
recent	kürzlich, vor kurzem
refreshments	Erfrischungen
responsibility	Verantwortung
space	Leerzeichen
subscribe	abonnieren
terms of delivery	Lieferbedingungen
terms of payment	Zahlungsbedingungen
to type up	zusammenschreiben
toolbar	Menü
tremendous	enorm, sehr viel
trip	Reise
to underline/to underscore	unterstreichen
willow	Trauerweide
word processor	Textverarbeitungsprogramm

355638

B. Email English

The next day Emma receives the following response to her memo from Mr Jackson.

```
Dear Emma,

Thank you for the memo and the nice reception at Blum Music. There is only
one thing. It says in the memo that the terms of delivery and payment remain
the same. Could you please send me those terms again?
Thanks in advance.

Martin Jackson
```

8 Fill in the missing words in Emma's answer.

terms	*attached*	*hesitate*	*further*	*anything*

Dear Mr Jackson,

Please find ______________ the ______________ of delivery and payment. If there is ______________ else I can do for you, please don't ______________ to contact me.

Have a good week ______________ .

Emma

Attention!
As you can see Emma did not use a traditional closing phrase. That is something many people do when they are corresponding with others on a regular basis. However, some kind of closing remark is usually used.

9 Sort the opening and closing phrases of letters and emails from very formal too informal.

Opening	Closing
___ Dear Madam or Sir,	___ Best wishes,
___ Dear Martin,	___ Sincerely,
___ Dear Sirs,	___ Best,
___ Hi there Martin,	___ Yours faithfully,
___ Dear Mr/Ms	___ Kind regards,
___ Hello Martin,	___ Regards,

Attention!
There are differences between UK and US greetings, of course. The most obvious is that UK English does not have a period after Mr and Mrs and US English has. Also, in some regions there is no comma after the opening and closing greetings. These things are not very important in everyday Business English. Simply copy the style which the person you are corresponding with uses.

10 Discuss in class or with a partner when you will need very formal phrases, and when informal English is appropriate. Consider, for example, who you would address with "Madam or Sir" and if there is ever a situation in business in which you would close an email with "Hugs and Kisses".

11 Unscramble the following phrases from the beginning of an email or letter.

1. writing we to that you are inform

______________________________ …

2. recently heard I about

______________________________ …

3. to our further meeting week last

______________________________ …

4. following contacting am you I for reason the

______________________________ …

5. for contacting thank you us

______________________________ …

6. your I address received from

______________________________ …

Attention!
In English emails and letters start with a capital letter after the opening greeting. All the example sentences in exercise 8 start with a capital letter.

12 Match the phrases with a suitable verb (more than one combination is possible).

We regret …	to announce
We are pleased …	to contact
I am contacting you	to request
We would be happy …	to inform
Do not hesitate …	to assist
I am writing …	to comply with
Unfortunately we are unable …	to complain
We are writing	to confirm

13 Rewrite the following sentences with would or could to make them more polite.

1. Send me the terms of payment and delivery.

______________________________ .

2. I can help you.

______________________________ .

3. Let me have the details of the meeting.

______________________________ .

4. When will you send me the minutes?

______________________________ .

Emma is having a very busy day at the office. She starts organising the Christmas party and a business trip for a colleague. In her lunch break she even gets a private email from her band mate Frankie.

14 Fill in the missing words in the three emails Emma has received this morning.

appreciate *concerning* *advance* *included* *accommodation*

From: nikhil.dasgupta@blummusic.com
To: emma.frey@blummusic.com
Subject: Visit to Munich
Send
from/CC/BCC

Dear Emma,

I am writing to you ______________ my trip to Germany from 9th January to 12th January. I would ______________ if you could book some ______________ for me and organise an itinerary; ______________ should be a plant tour and meetings with Mr Blum and John Miller. Will someone pick me up at the airport?
If there is any information you need from me, please let me know.
Thanks in ______________.

Regards,
Nikhil

mentioned *kind* *happy* *as soon as possible* *attachment* *further* *order*

From: bookings@finefoods-catering.com
To: emma.frey@blummusic.com
Subject: Catering Christmas party
Attachment: Pricelist_FineFoods.pdf, Order_FineFoods.doc
Send
from/CC/BCC

Dear Ms Frey,

We are ______________ to cater your office Christmas party on 15th Dec. In the you will find our price list and ______________ form. Please fax the order to us by 10th Dec latest. You ______________ in our telephone call that you will also need dishes and cutlery. Would you please inform us ______________ how many people will approximately attend to make sure that we provide enough table settings.

Have a good week ______________.
______________ regards,

Michael Inkling

355641

seeing	*work*	*about*	*know*

From: frankie_mornay@lmu-student.com
To: emma.frey@blummusic.com
Subject: Next rehearsal
Attachment: Tomorrow we'll survive.pdf

Send
from/CC/BCC

Hey Emma,

Here is the sheet music I told you ____________. I wrote the song and the band wants to rehearse it next time we get together. Does Monday or Tuesday ____________ better for you? I forgot. Let me ____________. Looking forward to ____________ you again. ☺

Cheers,
Frankie

15 Write Emma's responses and one email to her colleague Katherine, based on the German information given.

Nikhil

- *Gerne wird alles erledigt.*
- *Hotel oder Pension? Zentrum oder lieber ruhig?*
- *Besuch wird geplant: Besprechung mit Produktionsleiter George Lindner?*
- *Einladung Abendessen von Carl Blum und mit Kollegen, okay?*
- *Fahrer holt ihn vom Flughafen ab*
- *Abendplanung gewünscht? Tickets für die Oper, z.B.?*

____

____

____

____

____

____

Katherine

- *Idee für Lokal Besuch Nikhil Dasgupta?*
- *Dress Code für solche Anlässe?*

____

____

____

355642

FineFood Catering
- Danke für prompte Reaktion
- 30 Personen
- Getränkeliste fehlt
- Werden Gläser auch mitgeliefert?

Frankie ❤
- Super! Lied liest sich schon gut, toller Text. ☺
- Montag passt.
- Wegbeschreibung zum Bandraum wäre cool.
- Freu mich auch schon.

16 Write the email addresses.

john dot miller at blummusic dot com

rebecca underscore roth at L M U hypen student dot com

Martin dot Jackson at eventline dot {ko} dot U K

frank hyphen frey at online dot D E

17 Make up some email addresses and dictate them to a partner.

Emma has to set up some dates with various people and confirm some for Nadine. Before she does this she reads up on writing dates and times in English.

	British	American
spoken and very formal in writing	the 24th of September, 2012	September the 24th, 2012
long form	24th September 2012 24 September 2012	September 24th, 2012 September 24, 2012
numbers	24/09/2012 24/9/12	09/24/2012 9/24/12

All months (which begin with a capital letter) can be abbreviated with the first three letters, e.g. August - Aug.

For 2012 you can either say two thousand (and) twelve or twenty twelve. When you speak about a specific date you would use the first option, when you speak about a whole year in general you could use the latter.
e.g. "I met him on the 6th of April in two thousand eleven."
"The next US election will be in twenty sixteen."

Attention!
Dates up to the 12th of a month can be confusing if you use only numbers with slashes. Usually companies have a house style which you should follow, but for important dates it is better to write the long form.

18 Write down your birthday and the date of a national holiday in all possible formats. Describe the cultural stereotypes represented in the two visuals below.

British English

____
____
____
____
____

American English

____
____
____
____
____

Modal Auxiliaries

Hilfsverben haben im Deutschen sowie im Englischen die Aufgabe, Zeiten zu bilden und übernehmen die Flexion (Beugung), die zu der Person des Subjekts passt. Hilfsverben sind im Englischen "to be", "to have" und "to do". Sie werden nicht wörtlich übersetzt und haben nur eine grammatikalische Funktion.
e.g. I am going home. He has found his coat. Don't you agree?

Modale Hilfsverben haben eine Nebenbedeutung, die mitübersetzt wird. Sie werden immer von der Grundform gefolgt und verändern ihre Form nicht.
e.g. I can play the guitar. He should go home.

In der Kombination mit *have* gibt es Modalverben im Perfekt, e.g. "He should have gone home". Sonst werden in den Zeiten Ersatzformen verwendet.
can (können), *could* (könnten), *will* (werden), *would* (würden), *should* (sollten), *ought to* (sollen), *need to* (brauchen) werden im Großen und Ganzen wie im Deutschen verwendet.

Einige wichtige Unterschiede bei den Modalen Hilfverben sind:
- *must* entspricht *etwas zu tun haben* und ist sehr hart. Es ist besser, grundsätzlich die Ersatzform *have to* zu verwenden.
- *must not* heißt *nicht dürfen*; *nicht müssen* heißt *to not have to*.
- *can* steht im Englischen nicht allein, „Ich kann das" heißt "I can do this".
- *could* ist auch das past simple von *can*; um Verwechslungen zu vermeiden bietet es sich an, für *can* in allen Zeiten außer Present mit den Ersatzformen *to be able to* oder *to be allowed to* zu arbeiten.
- *shall* wird verwendet, um einen Vorschlag zu machen, e.g. "Shall we go out?". Sonst ist es selten zu finden.
- *may* und *might* gibt es im Deutschen nicht; sie bedeuten in etwa es *wird vielleicht, es wäre vielleicht, es könnte vielleicht*.
- *might* ist gleichzeitig Konjunktiv und Zukunftsform von *may*.

Attention!
Die Verwendung von *may* und *might* klingt idiomatischer und ist stilistisch besser als andere Konstruktionen. Vergleiche: It could perhaps be a good idea. It might be a good idea.

19 In a meeting Emma, Nadine, Katherine and Patrick discuss which fan articles Blum Music should offer to Eventline. Fill in the missing modals (sometimes more than one solution is possible).

Nadine: Okay, now that we've got everything, I think we ______________ start. Emma, ______________ you be so kind to take the minutes.

Emma: I ______________ be happy to.

Nadine: As you know, we ______________ to come up with some extra ideas for fan articles. ______________ we do a brainstorming first? Aw, again, there is no paper on the flipchart. Katherine ______________ you fetch us some from the office?

Patrick: It ______________ be a good idea to brainstorm the categories we are talking about. You know, stationery, household objects, clothes.

Nadine: Thanks Patrick, ______________ you give us some ideas?

Patrick: Well, I think Eventline is looking for something more original, so we ______________ forget T-shirts, but what about pants?

Katherine: Hm, we ______________ forget that we ______________ to mass-produce. Pants come in so many forms, fabrics and sizes ... But underpants ______________ be something we could look at.

Nadine: That's a nice start for a brainstorming session. Let's collect ideas and we ______________ discuss the pros and cons of the articles later.

After a long discussion, the team decides to go for customised socks, pillows and cups, so that fans can have their favorite lyrics printed on them. In the following weeks Emma gets quotations for each of the items and Nadine presents them to Martin Jackson. Mr Jackson likes the cups best, but decides for cost reasons to pre-select lyrics and only to offer this restricted collection.
Emma is very happy that the first project she has been involved in has turned out so well. She offers to help select lyrics as she is such a big fan of music and wants to get to know Blum Music's artists anyway. After a few weeks in marketing, Nadine gives Emma some very nice feedback. And so, enjoying her work, her life with roommate Rebecca and her band, Emma is settling in more and more and feels that it was the right decision to take this job and move to Munich.

Vocabulary

to abbreviate	abkürzen
in advance	im Voraus
to announce	ankündigen
to appreciate	zu schätzen
to attach	anhängen
attached	im Anhang
attachment	Anhang
to brainstorm	Ideen sammeln
to come up with	sich einfallen lassen
to complain	sich beschweren
to concern	betreffen
to consider	bedenken, einschätzen
customised (UK), -ized (US)	auf den Kunden zugeschnitten
fabric	Stoff
faithfully	hochachtungsvoll
to fetch	holen
hug	Umarmung
hyphen	Bindestrich
itinerary	Reiseplan
the latter	letzteres
to look forward to doing sth.	sich auf etwas freuen
lyrics	Liedtext
obvious	offensichtlich
pants	Hosen (US)
quotation	Kostenvoranschlag
regards	Grüße
to regret	bedauern
to rehearse	proben
to request	um etw. bitten, verlangen
to settle in	sich eingewöhnen
sheet music	Noten
sincere	aufrichtig
size	Größe
slash	Schrägstrich
stationery	Bürobedarf, Büromaterial
underpants	Unterhosen
unfortunately	leider

Idea:
Search for five favorite items in your home. Look up what they are called in English and then try to research when this kind of product was invented and by whom.

C. Getting to Know the Business

After a month assisting Nadine in marketing, Emma takes on some new responsibilities in purchasing and sales. She will help with offers, orders and invoicing. The heads of departments and her supervisors here are Margaret Wilson for purchasing and procurement and Sean Edson for sales and logistics.

C.1 Purchasing and Procurement

Margaret: For the production we usually have standing orders. We only change suppliers if there are quality issues. Cost-efficiency is a topic here at Blum Music as in every company, but we produce high-end products, so we choose suppliers for quality first and prices second. That is a luxury in today's business world. So, what we usually do is first place a trial order and if we are satisfied we order more. You will see that we have a lot of repeat orders, too. The production orders on call, because they don't have so much storage area. The parts are delivered just in time. All of this is done automatically by the system and is handled by the production. We only deal with this part of orders if there are new parts or new suppliers. We enter them into the system and then the production can work with the supplier and order numbers. Our daily business is cross-checking orders with invoices and passing them on to accounting; ordering supplies for the office; keeping an eye on new products that we might want to use in production, for marketing or for the label. Moreover, our department makes the enquiries for services that other departments might need and we take care of the specific terms and set up the contracts.

20 Which kinds of orders are there?

1. ______________________ Probebestellung
2. ______________________ Bestellung auf Abruf
3. ______________________ Dauerauftrag, Abonnement
4. ______________________ Nachbestellung

21 Write down in German which responsibilities Margaret has and which tasks she and her department fulfill.

- ______________________
- ______________________
- ______________________
- ______________________
- ______________________
- ______________________

Blum Music wants to order some new office furniture and Margaret assigns Emma the task of researching chairs for the office. The production has had a problem with temperature this summer, so she has to get three different quotations from companies which specialise in ventilation systems. And finally, Carl Blum wants to improve his Spanish, therefore Emma needs to find a language trainer.

22 Decide which sources of information are best for the three products and services Emma has to find. Can you think of other sources?

office chairs | ventilation system | Spanish trainer

yellow pages, catalogues, Internet, chamber of commerce, word of mouth, ...

Role Play

23 Emma has found two agencies which offer Business Spanish and one-to-one training in-house. She phones both. Role play both calls with a partner, change roles in the second call.

Call 1 and 2

Emma confirms: Business Spanish, one-to-one, in-house training
Emma enquires: trainer availability and possible start date, possible time slots, flexibility in training (weekly, biweekly, two times a week), material and training philosophy, price

Call 1 Emma – LangCom

LangCom offers: 5 trainers, substitute if regular trainer is unavailable
start date: next year, 10th Jan
time slots available only in mornings and early afternoons
regular weekly training sessions preferred due to organisational issues
training philosophy: what the customer needs is tackled in training
material: standard course books fitting customer needs
price: € 42/45 min

Call 2 Emma – ACR

ACR offers: 20 trainers, substitute if regular trainer is unavailable
start date: next month, 3rd Dec
all time slots available
regular weekly training sessions preferred due to organisational issues
training philosophy: ACR has fixed curriculums that the trainers follow
material: ACR material, included in price
price: € 43/45 min

Emma is not completely happy with any of these options. In the evening her roommate Rebecca tells her about a freelance Spanish trainer, Ms Fernandez. Emma calls her the next morning. Ms Fernandez seems more flexible than the agencies and also says that she does not use fixed material, but does on-the-job-training with executives.

Emma has found three companies specialising in ventilation systems and has called their contact people. As this will be an expensive order, everything needs to be very official and Emma sends out a letter to each of these companies.

355648

24 Match the parts of the enquiry to the letter below.

item numbers	*reason for writing*	*details of goods and services*	
requiring further information	*opening greeting*	*department or title*	*company address*
subject line	*recipient's address*	*complimentary close*	*date of letter*
appropriate ending	*amount of items*		

Blum Music4you KG
Senftlstr. 8
(1) ______________ 81514 München

(2) ______________ 4th Nov 201..

Ventilation Experts Ltd. (3) ______________
Bayerwaldstr. 20
81520 München

Ventilation Production (4) ______________

Dear Madam or Sir, (5) ______________

(6) ______________ Blum Music Ltd. would like to make an enquiry about optimising the ventilation system in our production. The improvement will include the replacement of some parts (see below) and an expansion of the ventilation. Please send us a quotation for the following items:

– spare parts	100-300-626 (7) ______________	x3 (8) ______
	100-487-242	x7
	600-939-022	x20
– max. 6 air vents	349-892-001	
– max. 12 valves	449-929-004	
– piping		
– man-hours for installation (9) ______________		

(10) ______________ Please advise us of your terms of payment. This is not a time-critical matter, however, we would appreciate if you could inform us about the possible time frame.
We are looking forward to hearing from you. If you have any further questions, please do not hesitate to contact us. (11) ______________

Kind regards, (12) ______________

Emma Frey

Purchasing and Procurement Blum Music Ltd. (13) ______________

Attention!
It is not common in written English to abbreviate verbs. Emails have changed this, but in letters or official documentation we still spell out *do not*, *is not*, etc.

▶ When Emma receives the three quotations she forwards them to Margaret and George.

25 Emma receives the following two offers for different office chairs. Fill in the missing words.

franco domicile	*delivery*	*concerning*	*invoice*	*enquiry*
forward	*payment discount*	*features*	*available*	

From: BusinessFurniture
To: emma.frey@blummusic.com
Subject: Office Chairs
Attachment: TX 10.pdf, General Terms and Conditions.pdf, Order.doc X

Send
from/CC/BCC

Dear Ms Frey,

Thank you very much for your ________________. Unfortunately, there are some difficulties in ________________ the model you are interested in, the TX 09.

We are pleased to offer you a ________________ on our model TX 10 due to a current promotion. This model is basically the same as TX 09, with some improvements ________________ the seating surface and two new ________________. Please find attached a brochure about the TX 10.

With the discount of 10 %, the price is only € 30 per chair more than the TX 09, at € 250 per chair. The TX 10 is available immediately, the TX 09 will be ________________ again at the beginning of the new year.

We deliver the chairs ________________ if the order comprises more than 20 chairs. For orders below this amount we charge € 0.70/ km ex works. ________________ is due 14 days after receipt of ________________. You will find our general terms and conditions in the second attachment. If you would like to order one of our models, please fill in the order form and fax it to us under 08731 555 920.

We are looking ________________ to hearing from you. If there are any further questions, please do not hesitate to contact us.

Kind regards,

Wolf Ganner

Sales Dep. Business Furniture
+49 943 555 876 23
wolf.ganner@businessfurniture.com

regard	*confident*	*competitive*	*impeccable*	*receipt*	*doing*

From: Office Furniture Plus

To: emma.frey@blummusic.com

Subject: Office Chairs

Attachment: Orderform.doc

Send

from/CC/BCC

Dear Ms Frey,

In _______________. to your enquiry we are pleased to inform you that the model you are interested in is available. The very _______________ price per chair is € 240.

As we are very _______________ in respect to our chairs' quality, we can offer you a trial period of 3 weeks in which you or one of your colleagues has ample opportunity to see the _______________ quality of our product.

Delivery cost amount to € 0.60 ex works, independent of the size of the order. Payment is due 30 days after _______________ of invoice, with a 2 % discount if payment is settled within 10 days.

We are looking forward to _______________ business with you. Let us know, if there are any further questions.

Regards,

Bianca Stein

Sales Dep. Office Furniture Plus
+43 824 555 321 04
bianca.stein@officefurniture_plus.com

Fax Order

26 Emma fills in the fax order for Office Furniture Plus. Label the order form with the corresponding terms in German.

Office Furniture Plus

Customer's Name (Plz Print):	Order Date:
Address:	
City, St., Zip:	
Phone:	* email address:
Ship To Name (Plz Print):	
Address:	
City, St., Zip:	Phone:

Requested Ship Date:	Ship Via:	
CC Name: VISA Master Card	CC # (Add Spaces)	
CC Bank:	Exp. Date – (mm/year):	CVN # (3 Digit #):

Quantity	Item Number	Item Description		Price	Amount

Remarks:		Subtotal	
		Discount	
		Total	
		Tax (CO)	
Customer Signature:		Shipping	
Clerk Initials:	Color:	AMOUNT DUE	

The Office Furniture Plus reserves the right to substitute out of stock items with a comparable in stock item & price.

355652

Comparing Adjectives

Adjektive (Eigenschaftswörter) mit einer Silbe werden mit den Endungen -er/-est gesteigert. Bei mehr als zwei Silben (und das gilt auch für Adverbien) wird mit *more* und *most* gesteigert. Das Gegenteil wird mit *less* und *least* (wenig, weniger) angegeben.

Beim Komparativ steht im Folgenden *than* (als).
e.g. Peter is nicer than Susan. Susan is more intelligent than Pam.
Pam is not the brightest student, but she is the most thorough one.

Attention!
than = als; then = dann.

Gleichwertigkeit wird mit *as ... as* (positiv und negativ) oder *not so ... as* (nur negativ) angegeben. Im Business English braucht man auch oft *the same ... as*.
e.g. Peter is as nice as Susan. Susan is not so intelligent as Pam.
This is the same chaos as last year.

Attention!
Viele Deutsche verwenden gerne *so ... as*, vergessen aber dann nach einiger Zeit, dass das nur bei negativen Vergleichen richtig ist. Ein typischer Fehler ist auch, dass statt dem as das an zweiter Stelle vollkommen falsche *like* verwendet wird. Es wird empfohlen, immer mit *as ... as* zu vergleichen, außer bei Sätzen wie "This is not so good.", bei denen kein Vergleichsobjekt folgt.

27 The Spanish Trainer. Compare the three options Emma has found and tell a partner about it. Which one would you choose?

	LangCom	ACR	Ms Fernandez
Organisation	5 Spanish trainers	20 trainers	1 trainer
Flexibility	regular weekly training only mornings and early afternoons possible	regular weekly training all time slots possible	can be arranged individually time slots need to fit Ms Fernandez's schedule
Cost	€ 42/45 min	€ 43/45 min	€ 40/45 min
Trainer	1 trainer, substitute trainer if possible in case of absence	1 trainer, substitute trainer guaranteed	1 trainer, no substitute
Material	standard course books	ACR course books	own material
Start date	10th Jan	3rd Dec	immediately

28 Emma talks to Carl Blum about the Spanish trainers. Complete the dialogue with the correct form of the adjectives given or appropriate words and phrases.

Mr Blum: Okay, this all looks quite similar to me. Ms Fernandez is a bit ____________ (cheap) ____________ the agencies. Do you think she is ____________ (competent)?

Emma: It is hard to say, of course, but I got the feeling that Ms Fernandez knows ____________ (good) what she is doing ____________ the trainers in the agencies, particularly ACR. For me, ACR is the ____________ (bad) option: they are ____________ (expensive) ____________ the others, but I read in a forum that they have ____________ (low) quality standards ____________ they say. LangCom made ________ good ________ an impression as Ms Fernandez. They seem to be ____________ (expensive) because they have an office to maintain. But they are ____________ (flexible) time wise.

Mr Blum: Well, I guess, I will book a first lesson with Ms Fernandez then, and leave LangCom as an option.

29 Word grid. Find the link words and phrases hidden in the word grid (all directions).

							H	F	N	Q	P	P							
					L	G	P	T	U	T	U	H	A	T					
			M	L	U	Y	E	O	A	R	Z	U	D	M	Z	A			
		H	N	O	L	Y	L	H	I	C	T	L	L	O	I	T	M		
		Q	H	S	G	A	N	R	J	N	I	H	Z	Z	A	K	C		
	Y	T	G	O	M	G	N	D	A	U	S	T	E	V	B	E	R	Q	
	L	O	N	U	E	H	G	I	B	L	S	P	D	R	R	B	C	T	
A	J	J	W	R	T	T	I	B	L	V	U	T	I	H	M	V	X	U	F
U	I	N	G	E	N	E	R	A	L	L	B	C	L	T	S	O	C	F	S
M	A	U	E	R	E	V	E	W	O	H	A	T	I	S	E	F	R	U	A
A	D	D	I	T	I	O	N	A	L	L	Y	F	E	T	O	O	M	E	O
Z	C	M	O	R	E	O	V	E	R	K	E	L	W	E	R	M	F	H	D
M	Q	I	V	T	D	Z	U	J	H	D	E	Y	S	Q	A	A	U	I	J
	E	W	N	I	U	D	M	C	I	H	F	U	L	R	O	A	P	D	
	E	R	O	F	E	R	E	H	T	G	A	Z	I	J	T	G	E	P	
		R	J	J	T	N	X	E	C	C	M	Z	G	M	G	S	V		
		N	U	N	O	T	N	J	E	F	I	F	S	Y	P	V	R		
			Z	X	I	O	Q	B	L	N	V	N	T	I	L	C			
					N	S	O	C	G	K	I	E	T	V					
							Z	Z	U	Y	P	E							

a _ _ in a _ _

ad _ _ _ _ _ _ _ _ _ _

alt _ _ _ _ _

b _ _ _ _ _ _ of

d _ _ p _ _ _

d _ _ to

f _ _ _ _ _ _ more

h _ w _ _ _ _

in g _ _ _ _ _ _

in s _ _ _ _ of

m _ _ _ _ v _ _

n _ n _ _ _ _ _ _ ss

pa _ _ _ _ _ _ _ _ _ ly

sum _ _ _ _ _ _ _ _

t _ ere _ _ _ _

y _ _

Vocabulary

additionally	zusätzlich
to advise	raten, anweisen
air vent	Belüfter, Ventilator
all in all	alles in allem
amount due	fälliger Betrag
ample	ausreichend
to appreciate	schätzen, würdigen
biweekly	vierzehntägig
brochure	Prospekt, Broschüre
chamber of commerce	Handelskammer
competitive	ehrgeizig, hier: wettbewerbsfähig
to comprise	umfassen, beinhalten
concerning	betreffend
confident	zuversichtlich, selbstbewusst
contract	Vertrag
cost-efficiency	Kosteneffizienz, Kosteneinsparung
to cross check	überprüfen (im Vergleich)
curriculum	Lehrplan, Kursplan
delivery	Lieferung
despite	trotz
discount	Rabatt
due to (plus noun)	wegen
enquiry (UK), inquiry (US)	Anfrage, Angebotsanfrage
executive	Manager (leitend)
expansion	Erweiterung, Ausbau
ex works	ab Werk
franco domicile	frei Haus
freelance	selbständig
general terms and conditions	Allgemeine Geschäftsbedingungen (AGBs)
good	Ware
to handle	bearbeiten, erledigen
high-end	hochwertig, teuer
however	jedoch
impeccable	perfekt, makellos
to improve	verbessern
in regard to	in Bezug auf, bezogen auf
in respect to	in Bezug auf, bezogen auf
in spite of	trotz
in-house	in der Firma
item number	Artikelnummer
just in time	Just-in-Time System (Anlieferung kurz vor Zeitpunkt der Verarbeitung)
label	hier: Musiklabel
man-hours	Arbeitsstunden
on call order	Bestellung auf Abruf
one-to-one training	Einzeltraining
order number	Bestellnummer, Artikelnummer
piping	Rohrleitungen
procurement	Beschaffung

promotion	Werbeaktion
receipt of invoice	Erhalten der Rechnung
remark	Anmerkung
repeat order	Nachbestellung
seating surface	Sitzfläche
service	Dienstleistung
shipping	Transport
spare part	Ersatzteil
standing order	Dauerauftrag, Abonnement
storage	Lager
subject	Betreff
substitute	Ersatz
subtotal	Zwischensumme
supplier	Zulieferer
to tackle	behandeln, sich kümmern um (ein Thema)
tax	Steuer
therefore	somit
time frame	Zeitrahmen
time slot	Zeitraum (im Kalender)
time-critical	dringend
total	Summe
training on the job	Lernen im Job
trial order	Probebestellung
valve	Ventil
ventilation	Belüftung
word of mouth	mündlich; hier: mündliche Empfehlung
yellow pages	Gelbe Seiten
ZIP code	Postleitzahl

C.2 Sales and Logistics

Sean: Obviously we sell our products, which are, as you know, guitars. The label and concert agency take care of their own sales, but logistics are responsible for shipping CDs and dispatching tickets. We organise transport for the guitars and the CDs. We sometimes negotiate prices for the guitars with our retailers, most of the time we have fixed prices and only offer discounts for big orders. Most of the negotiation is about the terms of delivery and payment. The invoicing is done by accounting, but we have to enter the information into the system. Further, and that is the less fun part, we deal with customer complaints. The supply chain is a responsibility of procurement, but stock control is of course a part of our work.

30 Write down in German which responsibilities Sean has and which tasks he and his department fulfill.

- ____
- ____
- ____
- ____
- ____
- ____
- ____

The warehouse and stock control

31 Emma brushes up on her warehouse English. Listen to the audio file on BBC English and find out what went wrong. http://www.bbc.co.uk/worldservice/learningenglish/general/englishatwork/2012/04/120411_english_at_work_episode_9_story.shtml

32 Match the headlines with the categories. Then label the words and phrases with their German equivalents.

Goods that are in stock	Other terms for delivery note	Terms for stock control
Equipment and places in a warehouse	Ways to pick goods	How to pack units
Warehouse owners	Things you do with goods	

(1) ______________________
- bill of lading ______________________
- delivery slip ______________________
- delivery ticket ______________________
- bill of delivery ______________________
- packing list ______________________

(2) ______________________
- manufacturer ______________________
- importer ______________________
- exporter ______________________
- wholesaler ______________________
- transport businesses ______________________

(3) ______________________
- work in progress ______________________
- consumables ______________________
- finished goods ready for sale ______________________
- raw material and components ______________________
- packing material ______________________

(4) ______________________
- picking ______________________
- checking ______________________
- labeling ______________________
- packing ______________________
- loading ______________________
- unloading ______________________
- dispatching ______________________
- tracing ______________________

(5) ______________________
- retrieval system ______________________
- pick-by-voice ______________________
- pick-by-light ______________________
- pick-by-paper ______________________
- pick-by-vision ______________________
- pick-by-barcode ______________________

(6) ______________________
- maximum stock level ______________________
- re-order level ______________________
- lead time ______________________
- minimum stock level ______________________
- buffer stock ______________________

(7) ______________________
- container ______________________
- cargo ______________________
- pallet ______________________
- pallet rack ______________________
- lane ______________________
- swap body ______________________
- box ______________________

(8) ______________________
- loading dock ______________________
- crane ______________________
- fork lift ______________________
- shelves ______________________
- goods receipt ______________________
- goods issue ______________________

355658

33 Research Incoterms on the Internet and explain the table below in German. Which Incoterm is most favorable for the buyer and which for the seller?

INCOTERMS® 2010 RULES CHART OF RESPONSIBILITY											
	Any Transport Mode		Sea/Inland Waterway Transport				Any Transport Mode				
	EXW	FCA	FAS	FOB	CFR	CIF	CPT	CIP	DAT	DAP	DDP
Charges/Frees	Ex Works	Free Carrier	Free Alongside Ship	Free On Board	Cost & Freight	Cost Insurance & Freight	Carriage Paid To	Carriage Insurance Paid To	Delivered at Terminal	Delivered at Place	Delivered Duty Paid
Packaging	Buyer or Seller	Seller	Seller	Seller	Seller	Seller	Seller	Seller	Seller	Seller	Seller
Loading Charges	Buyer	Seller	Seller	Seller	Seller	Seller	Seller	Seller	Seller	Seller	Seller
Delivery to Port/ Place	Buyer	Seller	Seller	Seller	Seller	Seller	Seller	Seller	Seller	Seller	Seller
Export Duty & Taxes	Buyer	Seller	Seller	Seller	Seller	Seller	Seller	Seller	Seller	Seller	Seller
Origin Terminal Charges	Buyer	Buyer	Seller	Seller	Seller	Seller	Seller	Seller	Seller	Seller	Seller
Loading on Carriage	Buyer	Buyer	Buyer	Seller	Seller	Seller	Seller	Seller	Seller	Seller	Seller
Carriage Charges	Buyer	Buyer	Buyer	Buyer	Seller	Seller	Seller	Seller	Seller	Seller	Seller
Insurance						Seller		Seller			
Destination Terminal Charges	Buyer	Buyer	Buyer	Buyer	Buyer	Buyer	Seller	Seller	Seller	Seller	Seller
Delivery to Destination	Buyer	Buyer	Buyer	Buyer	Buyer	Buyer	Buyer	Buyer	Buyer	Seller	Seller
Import Duty & Taxes	Buyer	Buyer	Buyer	Buyer	Buyer	Buyer	Buyer	Buyer	Buyer	Buyer	Seller

34 Match the terms with the definitions.

1. carrier
2. consignee
3. forwarding agency
4. shipper
5. supplier

a. a company which loads the goods
b. a company which produces goods you demand
c. the company which expects goods
d. a company which organises transportation
e. the company which transports goods

Idea:
Watch the promotional video for AB Warehouse Inc. on YouTube and see how much language learned in this chapter you can find: http://www.youtube.com/watch?v=9aFqIKOIEiY.

35 Research the advantages and disadvantages of the different means of transportation. Look at the grid and fill in the information you find. Present your findings to a partner.

	air 	sea 	rail 	road 
cost				
travel time				
convenience				
restrictions in size				
nature of goods (hazardous, shape, etc.)				
availability				
reliability				
ecology				

36 Label the labels.

radioactive *flammable* *corrosive* *high voltage*
endangering the environment *explosive* *toxic* *health warning*

 (1) ______	 (2) ______	 (3) ______	 (4) ______
 (5) ______	 (6) ______	 (7) ______	 (8) ______

355660

Dealing with Complaints

37 Emma receives some calls from customers complaining about quality issues or wrong deliveries. Replace the phrases on the left with polite telephone phrases.

Attention!
When people are very angry the best way to calm them down is to make them feel that they are being heard. So stay polite and listen closely to what the customer needs.

Find out what the customer wants:

What do you want? ______________________

What is your problem? ______________________

I didn't get that. ______________________

I really don't understand you. ______________________

So, you say the problem is ... ______________________

Show understanding

Aha. ______________________

I hear you, you don't need to shout. ______________________

Sure, that's a problem. ______________________

Well, that's your point of view. ______________________

So you want me to ... ______________________

Find out details

What's the delivery number? ______________________

Send me the invoice. ______________________

When did you order this? ______________________

Hang on. I'll check this. ______________________

So the number was ... ______________________

Offer assistance

Okay, it's taken care of. ______________________

You need to talk to quality. ______________________

We hear that a lot. ______________________

That's not our problem. ______________________

Close the call

(in response to a thank you). Hmh. ______________________

That's it then, yes? ______________________

Hope there won't be any more problems. ______________________

Bye. ______________________

Attention!
If you do not have ideas for everything, go to page 115 and match the phrases given there.

Reminder Notices

38 Cross-checking sales orders and accounts, Emma realises that some invoices have not yet been paid. She drafts some reminder notices. Fill in the missing words.

mutually	*overdue*	*outstanding*	*account*	*ignore*

Dear Mr Smith,

Please note your ____________________ account balance of € 3,650 is still ____________________.
Please arrange payment of this ____________________ today or, if you cannot make full payment at this time, please contact us to make a payment arrangement that is ____________________ acceptable.
If payment has recently been made, please accept our thanks and ____________________ this reminder.

Kind regards,
Blum Music

immediate	*accept*	*queries*	*concerning*	*settlement*

Dear Sir or Madam,

We are writing ____________________ the amount of € 10,550 which was due to be paid on 08/06/201... and, despite numerous requests for payment, remains outstanding.
We would appreciate an ____________________ reply. Please organise for ____________________ of this account today. We ask again that if you have any ____________________ or are not able to make full payment immediately, please contact us.
If payment has recently been made, please ____________________ our thanks and ignore this reminder.

Kind regards,

numerous	*notice*	*specified*	*associated*	*commence*

Dear Sir or Madam,

Despite ____________________ requests for payment your account still remains outstanding.
We demand payment of your outstanding account or we will list your details with our collection agency as of 05/12/201...
If you wish to prevent this, please settle your account before the above date.
If this account is not resolved by the ____________________ date we reserve the right to ____________________ legal proceedings to recover the debt without further ____________________ to you, and you may be responsible for any ____________________ legal fees or collection costs.
If you wish to prevent this, please contact the undersigned as a matter of urgency and settle your account before the above date.
If payment has recently been made, please accept our thanks and ignore this reminder.

Kind regards,

355662

Sales and Offers

39 Finish the first half of the offer by completing the letter. Use the information given, the hints in the brackets help you determine where to insert which information.

Items: 3 acoustic guitars model GT 1
2 electric guitars model ET 6
Price: 2 % off list price; GT 1 € 1600/piece; ET 6 € 3500/piece
Payment: 30 days net, 10 days 2 % discount
Delivery: shipment via international forwarding agency, within 4 weeks, shipment costs € 300
Validity of offer: 25th Dec
Enclosure: sales brochure, catalogue, price list

Attention!
Note that in US addresses the house number is in front of the street name, and the city is followed by the state and then the ZIP code.

Blum Music4you KG
Senftlstr. 8
81514 München
Germany

15th Nov 201...

Craig Music Shop
205 Main Street
Sunnyvale, CA 94088
USA

Dear Mr. Craig,

Thank you very much for your enquiry. We are pleased to quote as follows. The requested goods are available. We can offer you both models at ______________________________ ______________________________ (price and discount). If possible, we consolidate shipment, maximum delivery costs ______________________________. The terms of delivery ______________________________ ______________________________ (delivery).
This totals to an amount of ____________________ (calculate the total amount).
______________________________ ______________________________ (terms of payment).
The offer is firm until ____________________. We recommend to complete your order with possible complements or accessories to avoid future shipping costs. For your convenience we have taken the liberty to ______________________________ ______________________________ (enclosures).

40 Complete the last part of the letter with the words from the box.

approval	*inquiries*	*confirmation*	*quotation*	*business*	*carefully*	*engagement*

We hope this ______________________ will find your ______________________. This offer is without ______________________. This offer is subject to ______________________. We assure you that your order will be dealt with promptly and ______________________.

We look forward to doing ______________________ with you. If there is anything we can assist you with or if you have any further ______________________, please do not hesitate to contact us.

Yours sincerely,

Sean Edson

Sales Manager
BlumMusic4You

41 Find the terms printed in bold in the word grid (all directions).

Sean takes Emma to a sales meeting, in which the latest sales **figures** are presented. At first the sales revenue is shown in a graph chart, in comparison to the original **target** figures. This is followed by a **bar chart** showing the sales **forecast** for the next year.
The sales **representative** discusses a few issues, such as making **distribution** more cost-effective and the distribution **chain** more reliable.
Finally, Sean invites everyone to provide some ideas on how to promote **retailer** relations. The idea is to send out a sales representative to all the shops with a special **promotional** package for the new guitar, which will be **launched** in March. Sean states that the most important task is to convince the retailer of its quality, since they are the link to the **customer,** the **end user**.

B	S	A	Z	V	I	U	C	R	C	T	S	E	U
N	Q	E	O	W	E	U	E	H	S	H	P	V	K
X	O	O	R	G	G	M	E	A	A	R	N	I	Y
T	B	I	M	U	O	O	C	N	O	I	N	T	C
R	N	G	T	T	G	E	M	M	D	Q	N	A	U
A	Z	L	S	U	R	I	O	E	T	U	I	T	I
H	R	U	A	O	B	T	F	T	Y	C	S	N	R
C	C	Z	F	U	I	I	A	D	Y	O	Y	E	S
R	J	E	T	O	N	R	R	I	E	Z	Z	S	R
A	T	K	N	S	G	C	J	T	Z	L	C	E	C
B	F	A	X	E	K	B	H	O	S	T	A	R	U
P	L	L	T	X	Q	Z	J	E	U	I	Y	P	B
R	E	T	A	I	L	E	R	P	D	L	D	E	Q
F	P	C	H	G	K	A	E	A	D	O	Q	R	S

355664

Quantifiers

Englische Zahl- und Mengenwörter (*Quantifiers*) stehen vor Substantiven und geben im grammatikalischen Sinne eine Menge an. Die Verwendung von *Quantifiers* unterscheidet sich oft stark vom Deutschen. Hier die wichtigsten Regeln.

much, many – little, few

Hier muss man den Unterschied zwischen zählbaren und unzählbaren Nomen kennen. Normalerweise sind Nomen zählbar, e.g. one car, two cars; two people, three people. Dann werden sie mit many (viele) und few (wenige) näher bestimmt, e.g "There were many cars." "There were few people."

Unzählbare Nomen sind oft Sammelbegriffe. Um z. B. *money* zu zählen, muss man *coins* oder *bank notes* zählen, oder eine Währungseinheit verwenden; man kann aber nicht sagen: one money, two moneys etc. Ebenfalls unzählbar sind Dinge, die physisch schwer zu zählen sind, z. B. *water* oder *sand*.

Zuletzt gibt es noch ein paar Begriffe, wie *information* oder *advice*, die im Deutschen sehr wohl zählbar sind, im Englischen aber nicht.
A little und *a few* werden genauso wie im Deutschen gebraucht.
"I have little money." = "Ich habe wenig Geld".
"I have a little money." = "Ich habe ein wenig Geld".
A few würde man als *ein paar* übersetzen.

some and any

Eine einfache Regel, die fast immer richtig ist, besagt: in positiven Aussagesätzen steht *some*, in Fragen oder negativen Aussagesätzen steht *any*. Ausnahme sind Angebote oder rhetorische Fragen.
Eine komplizierte Regel, die immer richtig ist, besagt, dass man, wenn man weiß, dass etwas vorhanden ist, *some* verwendet, wenn man es nicht weiß, oder sicher ist, dass es nicht vorhanden ist, verwendet man *any*.

Emma has spent a lot of time working these past months, but rehearsals with the band have been going really well. She really likes her band-mates, particularly Frankie. They have been rehearsing some great cover songs, but most of all Emma likes working on their own material. Frankie writes the lyrics and comes up with the basic melody and structure of the song. Then the rest add their ideas during rehearsals.

42 Choose the correct word.

Emma: I love rehearsing with you so much/many. The new song is awesome. Do you have some/any idea how long I have been searching for a band like this.

Frankie: Haha, no, but I guess there weren't too much/many bands you liked at home?

Emma: Well, it was different and some/any people at my school had little/few opportunity to try new things, our music instructor was too strict. Anyway, are there some/any new songs to try?

Frankie: Yes, there are some/any, but not much/many. I didn't have much/many time the last weeks. I was much/many too busy earning a little/a few money. I need to buy some/any furniture, a new desk to be exact.

Emma: You need to buy a new desk? What happened? Some/any kind of accident?

Frankie: No, studying is what happened. There isn't much/many space on the desk, and much/many times I have to expand to my floor when I'm studying.

Emma: I see. Well, you should continue studying anyway. I like that you are smart.

Frankie: That is quite some/any compliment. Thanks. I like you for all kinds of reasons.

Idea:
Take a song that you like and try to write your own lyrics to accompany the melody.

Vocabulary

accessory	Accessoire, Zubehör
to accompany	begleiten
approval	Zustimmung
as follows	wie folgt
to assure	sicherstellen
bar chart	Säulendiagramm
bill of delivery	Lieferschein
bill of lading	Lieferschein
to brush up	aufbessern
buffer stock	Pufferbestand
cargo	Fracht
carrier	Transportunternehmen
charges	Kosten, Gebühren
to check	überprüfen
complaint	Beschwerde
complement	Zubehör
to complete	vervollständigen, ergänzen
confirmation	Bestätigung
consignee	Warenempfänger
to consolidate	konsolidieren, zusammenfassen
consumables	Verbrauchsgüter
crane	Kran
customer	Kunde
delivery slip	Lieferschein
delivery ticket	Lieferschein
to dispatch	absenden
distribution chain	Lieferkette (Verteilung)
enclosure	Anlage
end user	Endverbraucher
engagement	Verbindlichkeit, Verpflichtung
exporter	Exporteur
figures	Zahlen, Wert
to be firm	fest stehen, fix sein
fork lift	Gabelstapler
forwarding agency	Spedition
fragile	zerbrechlich
goods issue	Warenausgang
goods receipt	Wareneingang
graph chart	Graph, Liniendiagramm
hazardous	gefährlich
importer	Importeur
instructor	Lehrer, Anleiter
to label	kennzeichnen
lane	Gang
to launch	auf den Markt bringen, in Gang setzen
lead time	Durchlaufzeit, Vorlaufzeit, Vorhalte-zeit
liberty	Freiheit

355666

to load	laden, verladen
loading dock	Ladedock
manufacturer	Hersteller
means	Mittel
opportunity	Gelegenheit
packing list	Lieferschein, Packliste
pallet	Palette
pallet rack	Gestell für Paletten
to pick	wählen, auswählen, aussuchen
pick-by-...	Kommissionierung durch ...
promotional	Werbe-
to recommend	empfehlen
re-order level	Bestand sollte mit Nachbestellung aufgefüllt werden.
restriction	Einschränkung
retailer	Verkäufer (Laden)
retrieval system	Abfragesystem
revenue	Umsatz
sales representative	Vertriebsperson
shipper	Verlader
shipping	Transport, Versand
smart	klug, gescheit
stock	Lager
stock level	Bestand
supply chain	Lieferkette (Belieferung)
swap body	Wechselaufbau, Wechselbehälter
target	Ziel
to total	gesamt ausmachen
toxic	giftig
to trace	verfolgen (Spur)
to unload	ausladen, abladen
validity	Gültigkeit
wholesaler	Großhändler
work in progress	laufende Arbeiten

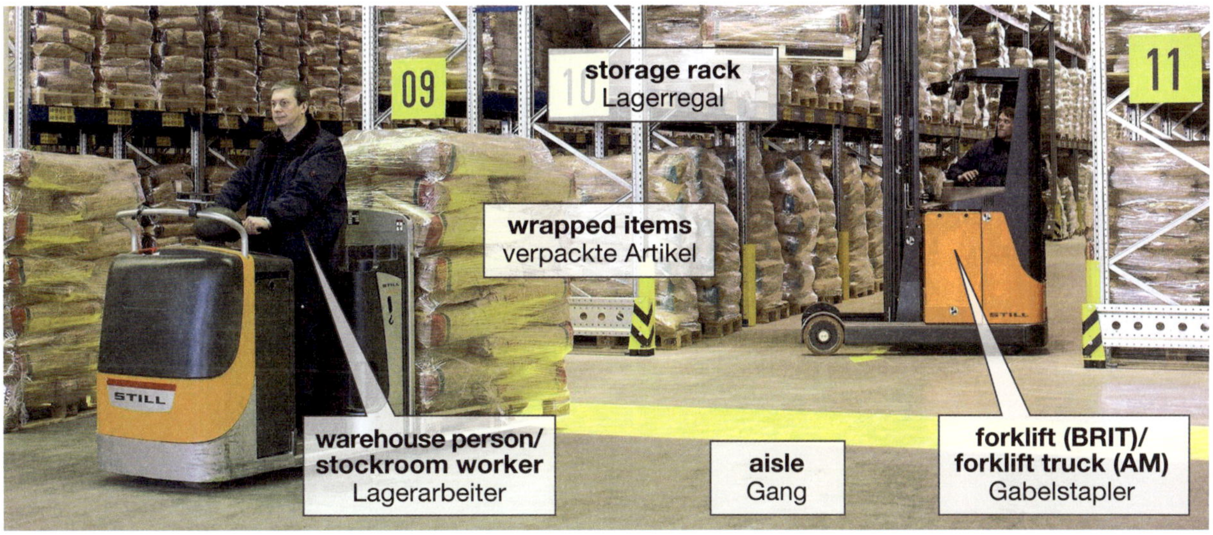

43 Doing Business

Across:

4 – to ensure that enough but not too much of a good is stored
7 – plans or an agenda for travelling
9 – you get this when you forgot something
12 – two people trying to make a deal lead this
14 – money the government gets from you
16 – to get something
18 – when something went wrong you...
19 – sourcing and purchasing together

Down:

1 – how much something will cost
2 – a vehicle used in a storage area
3 – a drink
4 – a company which produces goods you demand
5 – the words of a song
6 – happening at the moment
8 – the money made by a company without deductions
10 – without much strength or power
11 – bill of lading
13 – in a letter it is enclosed, in an email it is ...
15 – when you get 2 % off, you get a ...
17 – to include, to entail

355668

Starting a career

unit 4

In this unit, you will learn:

- How to chair a meeting
- How to negotiate, agree and disagree politely
- About contracts
- How to compare options
- How to give a presentation
- How to describe a graph
- How to talk about numbers and figures
- How to give directions
- About intercultural aspects in business
- About appraisal reports and feedback
- How to organise travelling abroad
- How to fill in forms
- Useful words and phrases for travelling
- Food and restaurant English
- How to report speech
- About conditional sentences
- When to use a gerund and when an infinitive

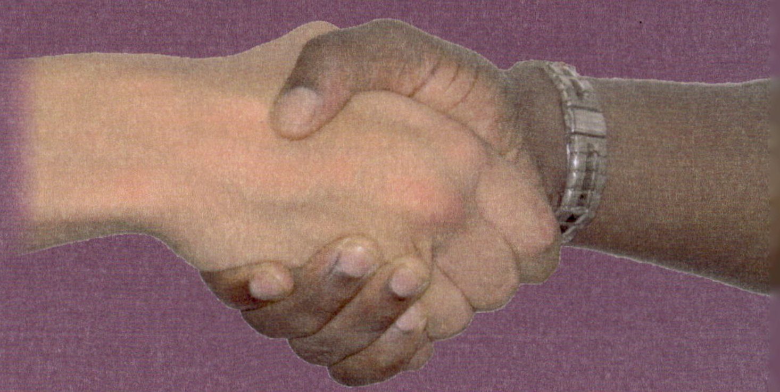

A.1 Meetings

Half a year later, Emma has got to know the company very well. She is now given her own projects in sales and marketing. One of her projects has been organising this year's trade fairs. The production of marketing material is, of course, outsourced to an agency, but it has been Emma's responsibility to provide them with the necessary content, choose visuals and decide which layout best fits the company's sales strategy. For the international trade fairs the material and exhibition is in English, but now Emma is planning the details for a fair in Spain, and wants to produce some brochures in Spanish.
Emma is meeting with the agency's graphic designer Tony, who she has got to know quite well, to talk about the details of the brochure. Nadine Summers is joining the meeting. They discuss the brochure and where to print it.

1 Choose the appropriate sentences Emma uses to chair the meeting, corresponding to the register (which is: good business relationship, first-name basis, 3 people in the room).

1 Right, shall we get started?
2 Ladies and Gentleman, may I open this meeting now? ☐

3 Would anybody wish to add another item to the agenda?
4 We've got a lot to talk about. Anything you would like to add to the agenda? ☐

5 I'll take some notes and send them to you afterwards.
6 Nadine has volunteered to keep the minutes. ☐

7 Okay, we have to decide a few things concerning the Spanish brochure.
8 The reason for our gathering is to decide on the Spanish brochure. ☐

9 I'd like to begin by congratulating Tony on his performance.
10 Thank you Tony for the drafts you've come up with. ☐

11 First Tony is going to give us a short presentation of the brochures.
12 Tony, could you first show us your rough copies? ☐

13 Nadine, what do you think?
14 I would like to invite Nadine Summers to present her views on this. ☐

15 It looks as if we have a consensus.
16 It seems we can agree on this one. ☐

17 I would like to proceed to the printing process.
18 Let's move on to the printing process. ☐

19 If nobody has any objections, I propose we postpone this decision until we have got all the quotations.
20 Perhaps we should come back to this when we've got all the details. ☐

21 To summarise I think we are in agreement on the layout. The printing details will be decided at a later point.
22 To sum up, we choose this layout, and the printing details we'll discuss later. ☐

23 Well, I think we've covered everything. Let's call it a day.
24 If nobody has anything to add I'd like to bring this meeting to an end. ☐

355670

2 For each situation above, come up with two other ways of expressing the same idea, one formal and one informal phrase.

1 ______
2 ______
3 ______
4 ______
5 ______
6 ______
7 ______
8 ______
9 ______
10 ______
11 ______
12 ______
13 ______
14 ______
15 ______
16 ______
17 ______
18 ______
19 ______
20 ______
21 ______
22 ______
23 ______
24 ______

Attention!
The Internet can help you with ideas for this exercise, if you enter "chairing a meeting phrases" in a search engine.
You can find more phrases at
http://mybusinessenglish.com/essential-meeting-phrases/or http://www.linguarama.com/ps/quality-themed-english/chairing-a-meeting.htm.

Some pages even offer exercises, such as
http://www.business-spotlight.de/language-skills/business-skills/chairing-a-meeting or http://www.bbc.co.uk/worldservice/learningenglish/business/talkingbusiness/unit2meetings/1agenda.shtml.

And some give more general advice, such as http://www.meetingwizard.org/meetings/chairing-a-meeting.cfm or
http://www.tefl.net/esl-articles/chairperson.htm.

3 Two days later, Tony calls Emma to talk about the printing process. Bring the call into the correct order.

___ **Tony:** Bye.

___ **Emma:** Yes, I'll call you as soon as I've heard back regarding the text. Bye.

___ **Tony:** Yes, I found a solution. I'm ready to go. Will you organise the shipping? After all, you are the principal ... Or shall I?

___ **Emma:** Alright, if you say so. When is the deadline for the data transfer to the German printers?

___ **Tony:** It seems printing the brochures here in Munich and shipping them is cheaper than printing them in Spain.

___ **Emma:** Hello Tony. How are you?

___ **Tony:** In two days, if we want to ship the brochures in time.

___ **Emma:** Okay, I'm listening.

___ **Tony:** Fine, thanks. I've got the details about printing now.

___ **Emma:** Seriously? How can this be? The shipment costs less than the Spanish printers charge?

___ **Emma:** No, thank you. I'll take care of it.

___ **Tony:** Hi Emma, it's Tony.

___ **Tony:** Talk to you later then?

___ **Emma:** Okay. I'm only waiting for a feedback on the Spanish translation. Have you taken care of our problem with the logo colours? You know it's important – corporate identity.

___ **Tony:** Yes, all the quotations from the Spanish printers were much higher than what I estimate the German printers will charge plus the freight cost.

4 Write an email to a forwarding agency, requesting the information given in German.

5.000 Prospekte, München-Madrid
Lieferung max. 4 Tage, Lieferung direkt zur Messe
Kosten? – Konditionen? – Zahlung?

From:	emma.frey@blummusic.com	
To:	logistics@freightforwarding.com	Send
Subject:	Shipment brochures	from/CC/BCC

Dear Sir or Madam,

____

____

____

____

____

____

____

____

Kind regards,
Emma Frey

355672

Emma has had the German brochure translated by a professional translation agency. However, she had a strange feeling about it and as she trusts her gut, she has asked Ms Fernandez, the Spanish trainer, to have a look at the text. And indeed, Ms Fernandez tells her that the translation is sloppy and does not sound like marketing material should. Emma calls the agency in for a meeting – they send in José Velasquez – and asks Ms Fernandez to join as well.

5 Read the dialogue and then try to express the italicised words or phrase them more politely.

Emma: Good morning everyone. As I have already *told you* on the phone we are *unhappy* with the texts you have translated.

José: *And what's the problem?*

Emma: Ms Fernandez *is here for this. Can you explain* what you found *so horrid regarding* the texts?

Ms Fernandez: *Yes.* Mr Velasquez, *I found many* spelling mistakes. *And also* some structural *problems* with the sentences. *And the language, it will not be very appealing* to a Spanish audience.

José: *Hm. That's* a matter of taste.

Emma: *Now ... The more important issue is* that there are mistakes in the copy you gave us.

José: *Okay, okay.* I *don't know* what happened here, but *I guess you didn't* use the final version.

Emma: *No*, I've already looked into that and I can say for sure that I used the last version I received from you.

José: Then *I don't know. I say*, we will get back to you with a proof-read version.

Emma: *You* know it is rather urgent and *I want* to have a second opinion. Ms Fernandez *will you* proof-read that for us again?

Ms Fernandez: *Yes.*

Emma: *You must see*, Mr Velasquez that we will have to consider cutting your payment due to insufficient quality if this version is not better.

José: *That is* stipulated differently in our contract. *Ms Fernandez, you are not a translation or marketing expert.*

Emma: *Now, now. We don't have the time* to discuss the register and style of the text anyway. The deadline for the printer is tomorrow. *Just deal* with the general correctness of the language, and we will pay the full amount. *There is* a clause in our contract allowing for such a deduction if the quality is not sufficient.

José: *Aha. Well, we will improve* the text and we will also revise the language one more time.

Emma: Thank you very much.

6 Read the dialogue and then identify the different strategies the participants use to make their language more polite and diplomatic.

Emma: Good morning everyone. As I have already indicated on the phone we are not quite happy with the texts you have translated. (1)

José: Well, what exactly seems to be the problem? (2)

Emma: Not to put you on the spot here, Ms Fernandez, but could you please explain again what you found to be a bit off with the texts? (3)

Ms Fernandez: Certainly. Mr Velasquez, I'm afraid I found rather a lot of spelling mistakes. (4) And there are also some structural issues with the sentences, aren't there? (5) And to be honest the language, well, do you think it will be very appealing to a Spanish audience? (6)

José: I can see what you are saying, but isn't that rather a matter of taste? (7)

Emma: If I may … isn't the more important issue that there are mistakes in the copy you gave us? (8)

José: Indeed, you are right. (9) I cannot be sure what happened here, but maybe it wasn't the final version that was used? (10)

Emma: Actually, I've already looked into that and I can say for sure that I used the last version I received from you. (11)

José: Then I'm afraid I cannot give you a definite answer. (12) Could I suggest that we will get back to you with a proof-read version? (13)

Emma: Yes, but you know it is rather urgent and in fact I would like to have a second opinion. (14) Ms Fernandez would you please proof-read that for us again? (15)

Ms Fernandez: Yes, of course. (16)

Emma: I hope you understand, Mr Velasquez that we will have to consider cutting your payment due to insufficient quality if this version is not better. (17)

José: Isn't that stipulated differently in our contract? (18) Frankly, Ms Fernandez, you are not a translation or marketing expert, are you? (19)

Emma: If I could just interrupt here. (20) Unfortunately, we don't have the time to discuss the register and style of the text anyway. (21) The deadline for the printer is tomorrow. If we could just deal with the general correctness of the language, we will pay the full amount. (22) There is, however, a clause in our contract allowing for such a deduction if the quality is not sufficient, isn't there? (23)

José: It appears so. (24) Anyway, let me assure you that we will do our best to improve the text and we will also revise the language one more time. (25)

Emma: Thank you very much.

Write down the sentence numbers behind the techniques for diplomatic language.

Agreeing politely: ______________________

Interrupting politely: ______________________

Introductory phrase or word (e.g. To be honest, frankly, I'm afraid, unfortunately):

____

Yes, but …: ______________________

can > could: ______________________

will > would: ______________________

want > would like: ______________________

am/is/are > seems/appears: ______________________

Normal question: ______________________

Negative question: ______________________

Question tag: ______________________

Inserting softening words (e.g. quite, rather, a bit, maybe):

____

Inserting a please: ______________________

Using a positive adjective + not: ______________________

Exchanging words and phrases for better sounding ones (e.g. problem > issue):

____

355674

7 Read the following definition of a contract from *businessdictionary.com* and match the German words with their English equivalents.

A contract is a voluntary, deliberate, and legally binding agreement between two or more competent parties. Contracts are usually written but may be spoken or implied, and generally have to do with employment, sale or lease, or tenancy.
A contractual relationship is evidenced by (1) an offer, (2) acceptance of the offer, and a (3) valid (legal and valuable) consideration. Each party to a contract acquires rights and duties relative to the rights and duties of the other parties. However, while all parties may expect a fair benefit from the contract (otherwise courts may set it aside as inequitable) it does not follow that each party will benefit to an equal extent. Existence of contractual-relationship does not necessarily mean the contract is enforceable, or that it is not void or voidable. Contracts are normally enforceable whether or not in a written form, although a written contract protects all parties to it. Some contracts, (such as for sale of real property, instalment plans, or insurance policies) must be in writing to be legally binding and enforceable. Other contracts are assumed in, and enforced by, law whether or not the involved parties desired to enter into a contract.

Source: http://www.businessdictionary.com/definition/contract.html

Vocabulary

	anfechtbar, kündbar
	annehmen
	Ausmaß
	belegen, beweisen
	bewusst, absichtlich
	bindend
	Erwägung, Betrachtung; hier: Entgelt, Gegenleistung
	erwerben
	freiwillig
	gerecht
	Gericht
	gültig
	implizieren
	Pacht
	Partei
	Pflicht
	rechtlich
	schützen
	unbillig (ungerecht)
	unwirksam
	verleihen, leasen
	Versicherungspolice
	vollziehbar, einklagbar
	Vorteil
	wertig
	wünschen, ersehnen
	Zahlungsplan

Reported Speech

Zur Verwendung der Zeiten der „berichtenden Rede“ gibt es auch im Deutschen Regeln, aber die tatsächliche Anwendung ist oft sehr ungenau. Im Englischen wechseln viele beim Erzählen auch in die direkte Rede, in der amerikanischen Jugendsprache hört man z. B. “And then she was like ...” als Einleitung. Es gibt allerdings klare Regeln, die im schriftlichen auf jeden Fall befolgt werden sollten. Die Grundregel folgt dem Gedanken: das Verb wird jeweils um eins in die Vergangenheit auf der Zeitschiene geschoben.

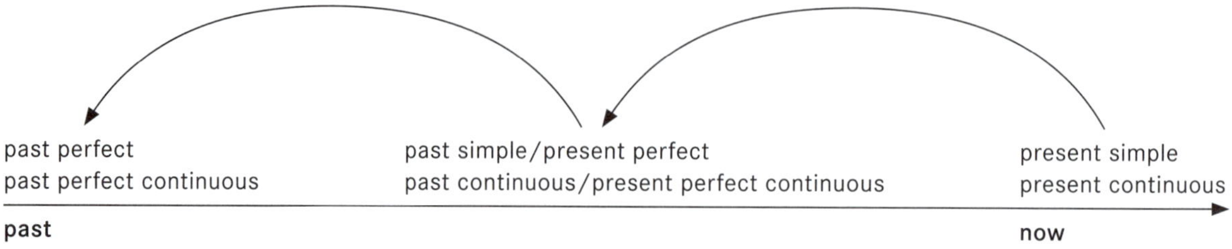

e.g. Peter: “I love coffee.” → Peter said (that) he loved coffee.

Kate: “I am leaving.” → Kate said she was leaving.

Peter: “I loved coffee when I studied.” → Peter said (that) he had loved coffee when he studied.

Kate: “I was leaving my office when the telephone rang.” → Kate said (that) she was leaving the office when the telephone rang.

Für die future tenses gilt: *will* wird zu *would* und *am/is/are* going to wird zu *was/were going to*.

Peter: “I will do this.” → Peter said he would do it.

> Attention!
> Don’t forget to change the personal pronouns, such as I to he/she, and demonstrative pronouns, such as this to that.

8 Emma reports the latest updates to Nadine. Change the direct speech to reported speech.

Tony: “I have taken care of the colour issue.”

Tony said that ______________________________ of the colour issue.

Forwarding agent: “It is going to cost about € 250.”

The forwarding agent said that ______________________________ about € 250.

Ms Fernandez: “I found many mistakes.”

Ms Fernandez said that ______________________________ many mistakes.

Emma: “I am not happy with the result.”

I said that ______________________________ not happy with the result.

José: “We will revise the texts.”

José said that ______________________________ the texts.

José: “We are working on it now.”

Josè said that ______________________________.

Emma to Ms Fernandez: I am telling you, I don’t trust them anymore.

I told her that ______________________________ anymore.

9 Emma and Nadine discuss the details of the exhibition in Spain. Fill in appropriate phrases including the words in brackets.

Nadine: The brochures are finished now. ______________________ (think) they are okay?

Emma: ______________________ (yes). But it ______________________ (might, idea) to engage one of our local business contacts or suppliers next time we outsource a translation. It ______________________ (disadvantage) if we don't have anyone associated with us who speaks the language well enough to understand the differences in style and register.

Nadine: Sure, but ______________________ (why) we are outsourcing, isn't it? Anyway, let's discuss the booth.

Emma: Okay, ______________________ (options). We've already booked a 10 X 10 exhibit booth, which includes a 6' table, two chairs and an information desk. The question is if ______________________ (add) a separate curtained 6 X 6 interview booth or not.

Nadine: I ______________________ (not, think) we should do that. There will be times when only one of our sales reps is at the stand and it would look empty if they vanished into the separated part.

Emma: ______________________ (right). So, that's a no. ______________________ (discuss) catering.

Nadine: What ______________________ (suggestions)?

Emma: I talked to some people at the fair and we basically have to options: traditional catering with canapés and a small lunch or tapas. Traditional catering is ______________________ (less) than the tapas, but I think the tapas are worth the additional cost. I hear that they are very good and it ______________________ (change) for our sales reps.

Nadine: Okay, then ______________________ (order).

Emma: The next point ______________________ (decide) is when to set up the booth. In Italy, the facilities were quite insufficient and a lot of equipment was missing, so the workers had to do a night shift. But if we set up one day early we will ______________________ (additional).

Nadine: My experience tells me that a night shift before the opening of a trade fair is the ______________________ (thing) to do. Stay with the schedule the fair sets up for you. ______________________ (anything else) we need to discuss?

Emma: One last thing, the floor. We ______________________ (between) carpets and laminate floors. I ______________________ (propose) to take the carpets, they are cheaper and will muffle the sound in the exhibition hall.

Nadine: ______________________ (agree). Great, it sounds as if everything is under control. Good work, Emma.

Emma: Thanks.

10 You are planning a trip to Berlin. In partner work or groups of three or four, discuss and negotiate the following:

- means of transport (advantages, disadvantages),
- how long to stay,
- what kind of accommodation (hostel, hotel, bed and breakfast),
- what to do once you are there (sightseeing or partying),
- what to take and who will take what.

You will find phrases to help you in your argumentation on page 119 in the appendix.

A.2 Presentations

Emma joins the quarterly sales meeting, where the latest figures and the sales forecast are presented. Afterwards there is always a strategy meeting.

Idea:
Im Band Informationsverarbeitung (Best.-Nr. 3568) der Reihe Kauffrau/-mann für Büromanagement wird ausführlich und mit anwendungsorientierten Übungsbeispielen auf das Erstellen einer PowerPoint-Präsentation eingegangen.

11 Fill in the missing words

commodities	*interest rates*	*target*	*economy*	*diversify*	*gross*	
demand	*break even point*	*figures*	*net*	*supply*	*debits*	*bookkeeping*

Sean Edson: Good afternoon everyone. Please let me draw your attention to the latest sales ____________________ shown in this graph. As you can see, we have not fully reached our ____________________. It is, of course, not a question of being profitable, the ____________________ has easily been reached. But the ____________________ is in a recession and ____________________ for luxury goods has decreased.

I would now like to show you general figures, fresh from ____________________. Here you can see ____________________ profit and after deductions the ____________________ profit. ____________________ are very low at the moment, so we should consider some investments. We have also settled all ____________________. One proposal was to lower the price for the new guitar – after all that is the basic rule of trading ____________________: ____________________ and demand set the price.

Anyway, we need to continue to ____________________ our products, but we have started doing that anyway, with the concert agency and the label.

12 Fill in the correct preposition following the example sentences.

a rise *from* 100 sales units *to* 150
to increase *by* 4 %
an increase *of* 4 % in sales

George Lindner: I would like to explain the rise ____________ unit cost ________________ € 500 ________________ € 550. First, there has been an increase ____________ 6 % ______________ energy costs. Then, we have needed more material for the new product. That means material costs have gone up ________________ 2%. And finally, labour costs have risen ________________ 1.5 % ________________ € 22.50 per hour ____________ € 23.20. With the slope ________________ sales, that means we have to think ahead in order to stay profitable.

355678

13 Fill in the table with the words below.

Verbs to describe an upward movement:	
Verbs to describe an downward movement:	
Verbs to describe no movement:	
Verbs to describe things happening at the bottom:	
Verbs to describe things happening at the top:	
Nouns to describe an upward movement:	
Nouns to describe an downward movement:	

reach/hit a low (point) · *skyrocket* · *a decline* · *an improvement* · *stabilise* · *a slope* · *an upward trend* · *slump* · *reach its/their highest point* · *go up* · *improve* · *soar* · *stay at the same level* · *decline* · *grow* · *decrease* · *plummet* · *edge down* · *a downward trend* · *an increase* · *a surge* · *rise* · *a decrease* · *reach a peak* · *a rise* · *increase* · *remain stable/constant* · *a fall* · *drop* · *growth* · *go down* · *be flat* · *edge up* · *stand at*

Attention!
You can emphasise the development by adding an adjective in front of a noun or an adverb after a verb, such as *gradual, considerable, significant, dramatic, rapid, sharp, slight, sudden, slow, steady.*

14 Label the graphs.

to fluctuate and level off	*to fall*	*to rise*	*to remain steady*
to reach a peak and then slope downwards		*to decrease and then recover*	

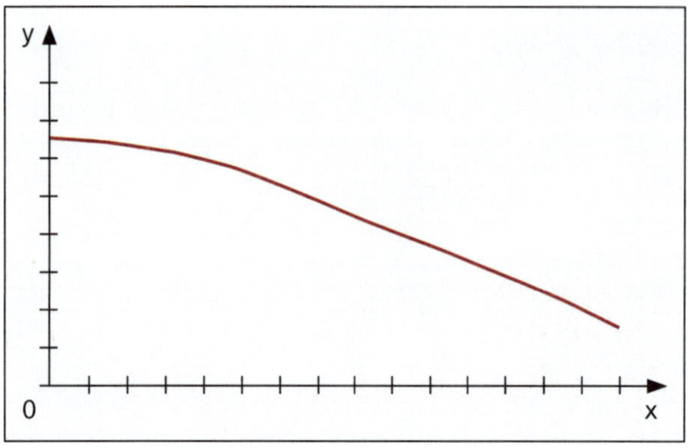

(1) ____________________

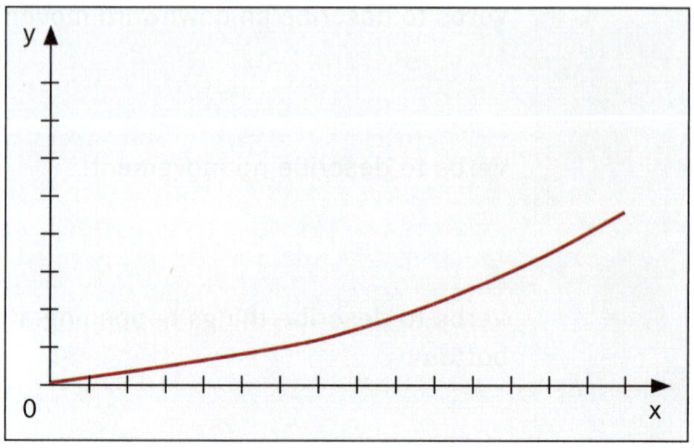

(2) ____________________

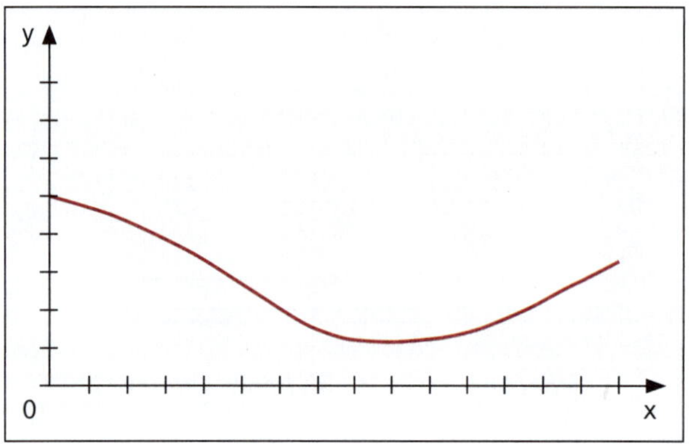

(3) ____________________

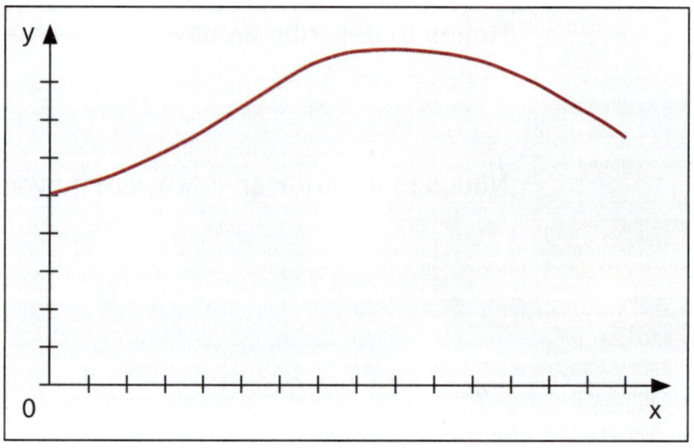

(4) ____________________

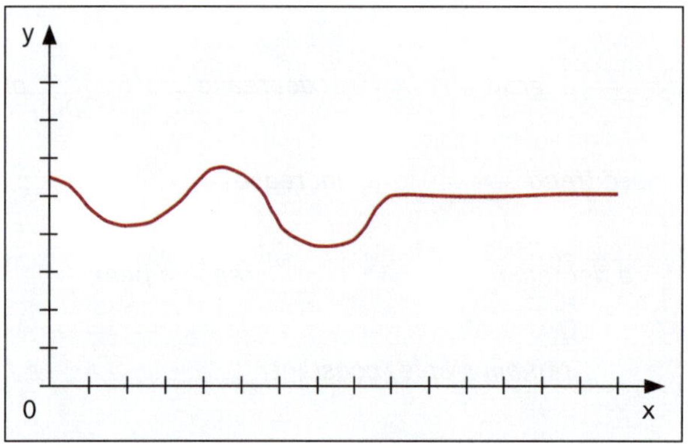

(5) ____________________

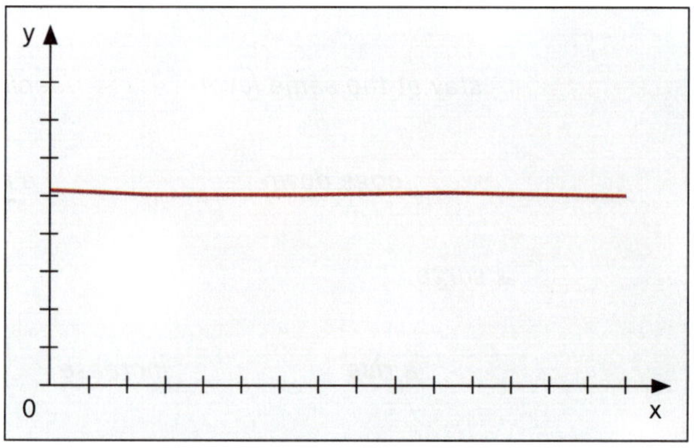

(6) ____________________

355680

15 Find the words in the word grid. Describe where you found them.
These words might help:

at the top, at the bottom, line, row, horizontally, diagonally, upwards, downwards
e.g. The word ... starts in the third line from the top, fourth row from the left, left to right.

O	T	H	N	F	I	R	O	C	K	E	T	S
S	C	O	N	S	T	A	N	T	G	V	U	P
C	L	M	P	D	P	C	H	G	Q	D	E	D
S	E	O	Z	P	O	R	D	F	E	V	S	E
J	F	Y	P	G	R	O	W	T	H	L	A	C
T	N	E	M	E	V	O	R	P	M	I	E	L
G	P	J	W	D	R	A	W	P	U	K	R	I
B	M	D	R	A	W	N	W	O	D	B	C	N
N	U	S	F	A	L	L	H	H	S	S	E	E
H	L	V	W	P	I	R	I	S	E	K	D	S
A	S	O	L	T	E	M	M	U	L	P	U	O
B	R	S	T	A	B	I	L	I	Z	E	G	A
G	X	L	E	V	E	L	D	G	N	U	I	R

constant
decline
decrease
downward
drop
fall
grow
growth
improvement
level
plummet
rise
rocket
slope
slump
soar
stabilise
upward

16 Go to pages 114 and 117 in the partner files. Take turns to describe the graphs shown there. While one of you is describing, the other one draws the graph. At the end of the exercise compare to what you have drawn to the graphs in the book and discuss the differences.

17 Label the various visuals used in a presentation, as seen on the next page.

map	*line graph*	*flow chart*	*table*	*pie chart*
organisational chart		*technical drawing*		*bar chart*

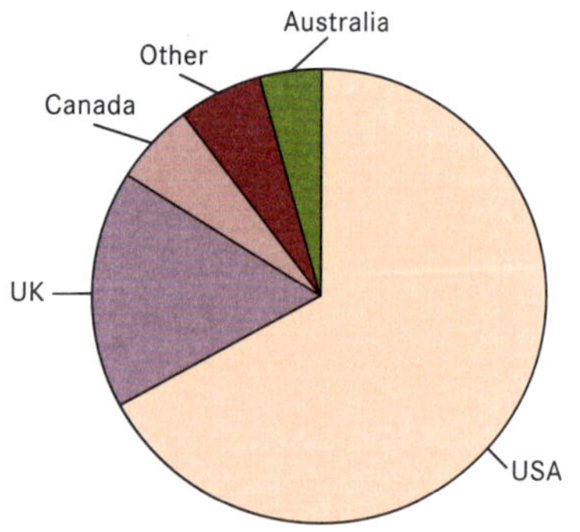

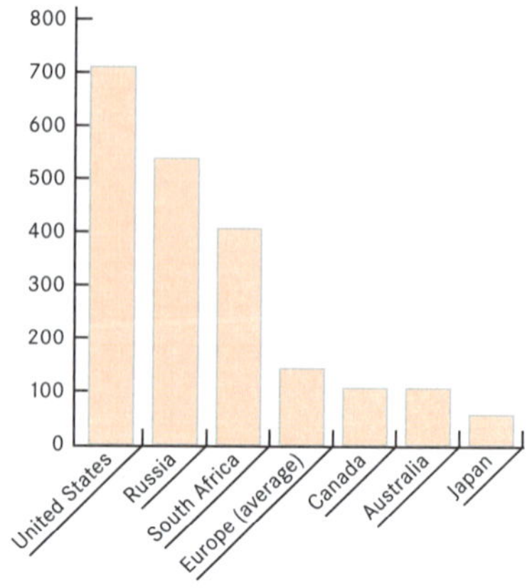

1. ______________________________

2. ______________________________

3. ______________________________

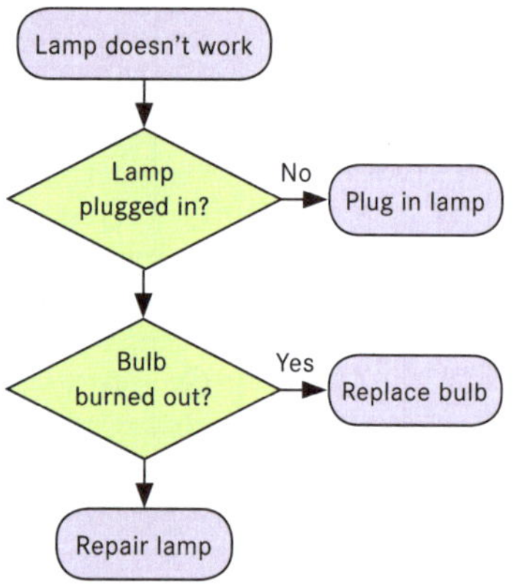

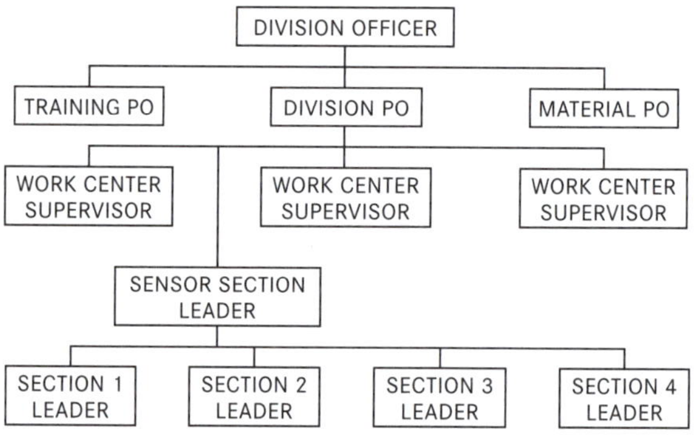

4. ______________________________

5. ______________________________

Summary				
Course Name	**Course Tutor**	**Room**	**Code**	**Fee**
After the Civil War	H. Smith	ZH 1	H27	$ 32
Poetry in the 1960s	C. Pattison	W 01	H28	$ 18
Foundational Texts	L. Unicorn	PT 07	H30	$ 18

6. ______________________________

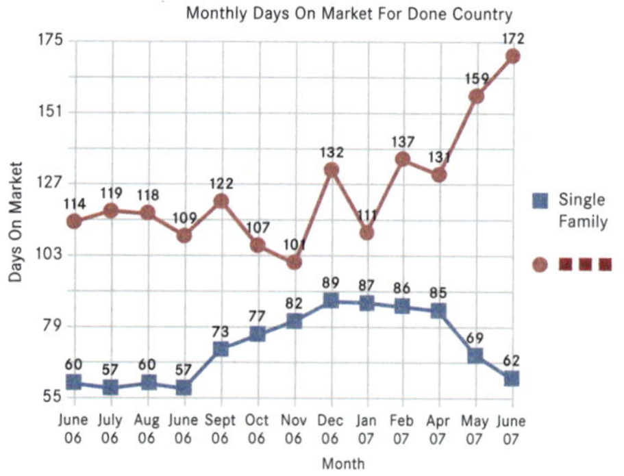

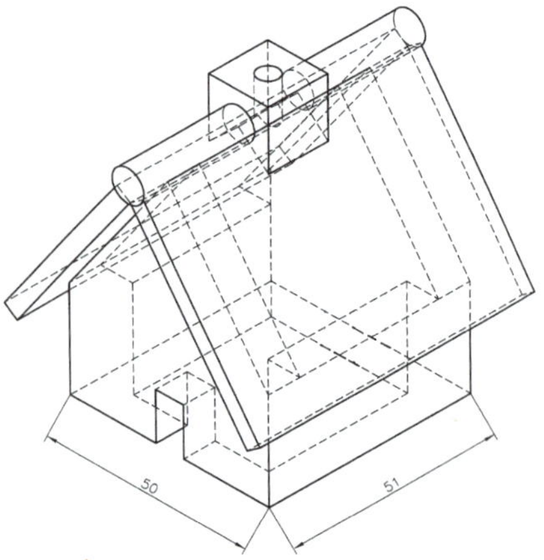

7. ______________________________

8. ______________________________

Numbers and figures

18 Complete the table.

1	2	3	4
	double		quadruple
a whole			
first		third	
	2nd		

19 Calculate the result and match the correct verb.

to add *to divide* *to multiply* *to subtract*

8 times 3 equals ______________. → ______________

430 plus 260 equals ______________. → ______________

49 divided by 7 equals ______________. → ______________

19 minus 5 equals ______________. → ______________

20 Write down the following numbers and figures as full words.

2,000,000,000 ______________

9 x 9 = 81 ______________

The booth is 10 m x 10 m ______________

The team lost 3 : 0. ______________

5 + 5 = 10 ______________

0° Celsius ______________

3 – 1 = 2 ______________

0049 555 893 ______________

$8\,^2/_3$ ______________

36 : 6 = 6 ______________

354,891,021 ______________

21st Dec ______________

09:45 a.m. ______________

3.873 ______________

$ 98.50 ______________

Attention!
In numbers the comma and the points are exactly the other way round than in German. And be sure to remember to say numbers after the point (decimal numbers) one after the other – you only say e.g. "twenty three" when talking about a value like a currency as in € 5.23.

If-Clauses

Die Bedingungssätze (if-Sätze) stellen immer wieder eine Herausforderung für Englischlernende dar. Doch eigentlich gibt es nicht viel zu verstehen, man muss nur die Formen auswendig lernen.

Immer gleiche Möglichkeit – Pattern 0
Der Pattern 0 bezieht sich auf Bedingungen und Folgen, die immer gleich sind. Dieses *if* kann man mit *immer dann, wenn* übersetzen.
e.g. If you cook water at 100° C, it boils.

1. Möglichkeit: die Bedingung liegt in der Zukunft – Pattern 1
e.g. If you study hard, you will pass the exam. → Wenn Du fleißig lernst, wirst Du die Prüfung bestehen.
Die Bedingung ist, viel zu lernen – und dafür ist auch noch Zeit – dann wird die Folge, die Prüfung zu bestehen, eintreffen.

2. Möglichkeit: die Bedingung bezieht sich auf die Gegenwart – Pattern 2
e.g. If you studied hard, you would pass the exam. → Wenn Du fleißig lernen würdest, würdest Du die Prüfung bestehen.
Die Bedingung, viel zu lernen, ist hier nicht erfüllt. „Wenn Du lernen würdest ... Tust Du aber nicht.“ ("If you studied ... but you aren't."); somit wird auch die Folge, die Prüfung nicht zu bestehen, nicht eintreffen. Viele Grammatiken stellen diesen Bedingungsansatz als nicht erfüllbar dar, das ist jedoch nicht ganz richtig, denn theoretisch könnte die betroffene Person lernen. Die Bedingung ist in diesem Fall einfach nicht erfüllt.
Es fallen aber auch alle nicht erfüllbaren Dinge in diese Kategorie, e.g. "If I were you." „Wenn ich Du wäre.“
Mit diesem Pattern haben Deutsche besonders deshalb oft Schwierigkeiten, weil im if-Satz selbst kein *would* steht, sondern past simple.

3. Möglichkeit: die Bedingung bezieht sich auf die Vergangenheit – Pattern 3
e.g. If you had studied hard, you would have passed the exam. → Wenn Du fleißig gelernt hättest, hättest Du die Prüfung bestanden.
Die Bedingung, viel zu lernen, wurde nicht erfüllt, also ist auch die Folge, die Prüfung zu bestehen, nicht eingetroffen. Es wäre anderes möglich gewesen, aber jetzt ist es zu spät.

pattern	if-clause	main clause
0	If you study hard, **present simple**	you pass exams. **present simple**
1	If you study hard, **present simple**	you will pass the exam. **will-future**
2	If you studied hard, **past simple**	you would pass the exam. **would + Infinitive**
3	If you had studied hard, **past perfect**	you would have passed the exam. **would + have + 3rd form (past participle)**

Attention!
Wenn der Hauptsatz an zweiter Stelle folgt, steht ein Komma; wenn der if-Satz an zweiter Stelle folgt, ist ein Komma erlaubt aber unüblich.

if vs. when
Der Unterschied zwischen *if* und when ist, dass *when* einen Zeitpunkt beschreibt, an dem etwas sicher passiert und *if* stellt eine Möglichkeit dar, die nicht unbedingt eintrifft.
e.g. Say hi to Tom when you see him. → Grüße Tom, (dann) wenn Du ihn siehst. (passiert sicher).
Say hi to Tom if you see him. → Grüße Tom, wenn (= für den Fall, dass) Du ihn siehst.

21 Rebecca and Emma want to redecorate their flat. Fill in the verb in the correct form.

Rebecca: Oh Emma, I have so many ideas! If we ______________________________ (be able to) afford it, I ______________________________ (turn) our flat into a palace.

Emma: Haha, Rebecca, I believe you, but we aren't.

Attention!
One of the sentences combines patterns two and three.

355684

Rebecca: Well, well. If I ______________________ (not, spend) so much on my wardrobe, I would have more money for this now. But if we ______________________ (think) hard about it, we might come up with some inexpensive versions of my ideas. For example, I would like to have some ornaments on the wall, but wallpaper is so expensive.

Emma: Well, if we ______________________ (buy) only wallpaper for one wall and ______________________ (paint) the other walls in a nice, matching colour, we will have a similar effect.

Rebecca: Good idea. What about space? If we ______________________ (move) the sofa this way, we ______________________ (have) more space.

Emma: Yes, but if we ______________________ that, we ______________________ (must) move the TV as well. I think, I ______________________ (like) it if the TV wasn't the centre of the living room anymore. It ______________________ (be) better over there, where the cabinet is now. We ______________________ (need) to move the cabinet if we ______________________ (want) to paint the walls.

Rebecca: Okay, that leaves decorations. I would like to have more pillows and stuff, but not the ones you can buy. If I ______________________ (can) sew, I ______________________ (make) us some personalised ones.

Emma: I will ask my mum if she wants to make some. If I ______________________ (pay) attention when I was little I ______________________ (can) sew now, but I hated it. My mum loves it, though.

Rebecca: Alright. It sounds like a plan. Shall we start by buying the wallpaper and paint?

Emma: Yes, but if we ______________________ (go) to the store by car anyway, we ______________________ (should) search for some fabric in a nice colour, too. I will take a sample and tell my mum which brand and colour we would like.

Rebecca: If I ______________________ (have) a mum like you, I ______________________ (let) her work for me all the time. Haha. Well, my mum has a lot of other qualities, though.

Emma: Your mum is awesome.

Rebecca: She is. Okay, if we ______________________ (leave) now, we ______________________ (get) everything today.

Emma: Hm. That's all great. But we will not be able to move the heavy cabinet on our own.

Rebecca: I have the best idea ever. What if we ______________________ (call) Frankie? It would be a good excuse to see him.

Emma: Okay, but only if you ______________________ (promise) to stop smirking like this.

22 Tell a partner ...

- about one thing you would like to change about a past event using if-clause pattern 3 to explain what would have been different.
- what you would do if you were a famous singer or movie star.
- about one thing you want to achieve and what that will mean for your life.

> Idea:
> The Internet can also be helpful in finding out what not to say. Go to http://www.huffingtonpost.com/2013/03/26/65-business-words-you-should-never-say_n_2956533.html to learn which business words to strike from your vocabulary.

Vocabulary

to achieve	erreichen
to acquire	erwerben
to add	addieren
advantage	Vorteil
agenda	Tagesordnung, Plan, Absicht
amount	Menge, Betrag
appealing	ansprechend
appropriate	passend
to associate	verbinden mit
to assume	annehmen
to assure	versichern
bar chart	Säulendiagramm
benefit	Vorteil
to be off	eigenartig sein
binding	bindend
bookkeeping	Buchhaltung
booth	Stand, Zelle
brand	Marke
cabinet	Schrank
carpet	Teppich
to chair	vorsitzen
to charge	berechnen
clause	Klausel
commodity	Handelsware
consensus	Konsens, Übereinstimmung
considerable	bemerkenswert
consideration	Erwägung, Betrachtung; hier: Entgelt, Gegenleistung
content	Inhalt
corporate	Firmen-
corporate identity	einheitliche Gestaltung eine Firma betreffend
court	Gericht
to cover	abdecken
curtain	Vorhang
debits	Schulden
decoration	Dekoration
deduction	Abzug
deliberate	bewusst, absichtlich
demand	Nachfrage
to desire	wünschen, ersehnen
disadvantage	Nachteil
diversify	sich breiter aufstellen, erweitern
to divide	teilen
draft	Entwurf
drawing	Zeichnung
duty	Pflicht
economy	Wirtschaft
enforceable	vollziehbar, einklagbar
to engage	miteinbeziehen, anheuern, verpflichten

equals	ist gleich
equipment	Ausstattung, Ausrüstung
to estimate	schätzen (eine Zahl)
to evidence	belegen, beweisen
excuse	hier: Ausrede
exhibition	Ausstellung
extent	Ausmaß
fabric	Stoff
facility	Einrichtung
fair	gerecht
figures	Zahlen (mit Wert)
first-name basis (to be on a)	beim Vornamen (sich nennen)
fitting	passend
forecast	Vorhersicht, Vorausschau
frank	ehrlich
freight	Fracht
gathering	Zusammenkunft
gross	brutto
horrid	schrecklich
to imply	implizieren
to improve	verbessern
to indicate	andeuten
inequitable	unbillig (ungerecht)
instalment plan	Zahlungsplan
insufficient	unzureichend
insurance policy	Versicherungspolice
interest rate	Zinsen
to interrupt	unterbrechen
laminate floor	Laminat
lease	verleihen, leasen
legal	rechtlich
line graph	Liniendiagramm
logo	Firmenlogo
map	Karte
matter of taste	Geschmackssache
to muffle (sound)	dämpfen (Lärm)
to multiply	multiplizieren

net	netto
night shift	Nachtschicht
objection	Einwand
organisational chart	Organigramm
ornaments	Schmuck
to outsource	auslagern
party	Partei
peak	Spitze
performance	Leistung
pie chart	Tortendiagramm
pillow	Kissen
to plummet	ins Bodenlose fallen, abstürzen
to proof-read	Korrektur lesen
proposal	Vorschlag
to propose	vorschlagen
to protect	schützen
quadruple	vierfach
rapid	schnell
to revise	überarbeiten
to rocket	in die Höhe schießen, abheben
rough copy	Entwurf
sample	Sample, Beispielstück, Teststück
to set up	aufbauen
to settle	ausgleichen, begleichen
to sew (spoken to sow)	nähen
shipment	Transport
significant	bedeutend
similar	ähnlich
sloppy	schlampig
to smirk	grinsen
to soar	fliegen
square	Quadrat
stand	Messestand
stipulated	festgelegt (vertraglich)
to subtract	subtrahieren
suitable	passend
supply	Angebot, Lieferung
table	Tabelle
target	Ziel
tenancy	Pacht
trade fair	Messe
urgent	dringend
valid	gültig
valuable	wertig
to vanish	verschwinden
visual	Bildmaterial
void	unwirksam
voidable	anfechtbar, kündbar
voluntary	freiwillig
to volunteer	sich freiwillig melden
wallpaper	Tapete
wardrobe	Kleidung

355688

B.1 Presenting your company to customers

Emma has been in charge of creating a new presentation for Blum Music. She uses power point, but is not quite sure about the formatting. She researches style guides and this is what she finds out:

Capitalisation: Titles and Headings

There are four possibilities:
1. Capitalise first and last word, everything but articles and prepositions (if not part of the verb), and common conjunctions (but, so, and, yet).
2. Capitalise first and last word, every principal words, and every word longer than three letters
3. Capitalise as in a normal sentence. (Nations, languages, nationalities, weekdays, months, God, I, names and brands)
4. Capitalise every word.

Idea:
Go to Grammar Girl's *Quick and Dirty Tips:* http://www.quickanddirtytips.com/education/grammar. Grammar Girl has a lot of interesting podcasts on problems you may encounter while using English every day.

Capitalisation: Bullet points

These are some general rules:
- lower case with single words possible
- capital letter with full sentence
- depends on punctuation (comma – lower case/period – capital letter)
- punctuation: use commas for sentence fragments or single words; nothing if informal; periods for full sentences
- introductory sentence can be with colon, comma or nothing
- use numbered points when there is no particular order (all capitalised)
- use lettered lists when there is a choice involved (usually lower case)

All style guides tell Emma not to oversimplify, since everything lower case is too informal; everything in capital letters is confusing and looks like shouting. Often this is a style choice, the most important thing is to be consistent throughout the presentation.
Bullet points are sentence fragments, and usually leave out articles and often subjects; there is often one verb for more points.

23 Capitalise these headlines from today's newspapers. Make a style choice and be consistent.

heart deaths: the curious case of the vanishing killer

__eart __eaths: __he __urious __ase __f __he __anishing __iller

a phone box in your garden

__ __hone __ox in __our __arden

brain drain as germans lure southern europeans

__rain __rain __s __ermans __ure __outhern __uropeans

Attention!
You should always try to use parallel constructions in presentations and generally in lists. There are many possibilities, but don't have a single word, a sentence fragment, a full sentence on the same slide and also try to be consistent within the presentation. Plus, be careful with noun phrases: Germans tend to translate compound words literally!

24 Emma gives a presentation about Blum Music. The company is a South African concert agency, Event Concert. Help her through the various steps of the presentation. Go to page 120 for phrases for presentations.

____

____.

(Welcome the customer, Mr Littfield and his two colleagues from the firm Event Concert.)

____

____.

(Emma introduces herself and the purpose of the presentation.)

____

____

____.

(First point: Blum Music's company structure and product range, visual: flow chart.)

____

____

____.

(Second point: company history, founded in 1977, expanded from there, music label founded in 1994, concert agency and marketing material added in 2002, subsidiary in Berlin founded in 2010.)

____

____

____.

(Third point: business opportunities and possible cooperation with Event Concert: concert tour of Blum Music artists, providing marketing material.)

____

____

____.

(Summarise: Blum Music successful company in the music industry. Cooperation with Event Concert desired.)

____.

(Invite questions.)

____.

(Thank for attention.)

355690

B.2 Intercultural aspects: Traditions, Social Codes and Habits in Business

Emma has been a bit nervous about meeting so many different customers from all over the world. She brushes up on intercultural differences to avoid big mistakes or – worst case – insulting a customer. However, with all her research she finds that most customers know German customs, too, and are just as willing to adapt or at least accept things as Emma is.

25 Discuss how the following aspects and situations in business are handled in Germany. Do you know how things are different in other countries?

sense of humour | *presents* | *small talk* | *saying hello* | *meetings* | *reserve or conduct* | *work hours* | *physical proximity* | *dresscode* | *social events* | *punctuality*

There is a big, but sometimes difficult difference between believing national stereotypes and acknowledging cultural differences. E.g. Germans are said to be punctual. That means that in general, it is customary in Germany to be on time and everyone knows this – it is a social code. But that does not mean that every German person automatically is punctual; that would be a national stereotype.

26 Divide into groups and research the intercultural differences of the following countries concerning the topics above on the Internet.

China Britain USA (East Coast)

South Africa France India

Idea:
Look around your class. Are there people with different cultural backgrounds?

B.3 Performance review

The time has come for Emma's first appraisal meeting. Like most companies, Blum Music has a performance rating that also has an impact on a possible future promotion – and of course on salary negotiations. Emma is quite nervous about it, but she knows that there is not actually any cause for concern. Rather, Emma tries to think about what she wants to do in the next year and where she sees room for improvement or development. She has to write a short report and will then meet with Meredith Williams from HR.

27 Match the heading to paragraphs A–E in Emma's report

accomplishments	*areas for development*	*summary of work*
cooperation with colleagues	*goals and targets*	

Emma Frey
Blum Music4You

Performance Report

A I started my job as an office clerk at Blum Music4You in October 201.. . The first three months I spent on getting to know the company and assisting in the marketing, the sales and the purchase departments. Since the beginning of this year I have been working almost completely for the marketing department.

B During my time in the sales and purchase departments I assisted with daily business: receiving orders and dealing with complaints, making offers and placing orders, and checking invoices against orders and receipts. Part of my responsibility for both the sales and marketing departments is to organise visits by customers and business partners. I have created a new company presentation for this. {...}

C I work very closely with Nadine Summers, who has taken on the role of a mentor for me. The team work at Blum Music in general is very good, the work atmosphere is excellent and all my colleagues are of assistance whenever I ask them for something. {...}

D While I was organising the trade fairs, I have started to consider acquiring another language. As Blum Music operates globally, I think this might be helpful. Another area I would be interested in is intercultural communication. While I was working for the purchase department, I encountered some difficulties with the SAP Program.

E My goal for the next year is to increase my contribution to this company. I am looking forward to my first business trip at the end of this month. One target is to improve my SAP skills and if possible take some training on layout software.

355692

Evaluation

- [x] OUTSTANDING
- [ ] Excellent
- [ ] Very Good
- [ ] Average
- [ ] Below Average

28 One week after handing in the performance report, Emma meets with Ms Williams. Read the conversation and then fill in the table on the next page.

Ms Williams: Hello Ms Frey. How are you? Please come in and have a seat.

Emma: Thank you.

Ms Williams: Ms Frey, have you settled in here? And in Munich?

Emma: Yes, I have. I like Munich a lot and I get along very well with my roommate. And I also like it here at Blum Music.

Ms Williams: I am glad to hear that. Well, let's get to the performance review, shall we? You have stated your accomplishments in the report, and I have to say – your colleagues have not only confirmed your good work, but many have told me what a friendly and helpful colleague you are. Your work has been very good, not flawless, of course, but that is mainly due to inexperience. Would you agree?

Emma: I guess that I am not always sure what to do in complicated situations, but Ms Summers has been a great help. And I am trying to learn ...

Ms Williams: Yes, Ms Summers has pointed out to me that you handled a difficult situation with a translation very well. Now, you write about the areas in which you would like to develop and some goals, but let me ask you first – what kind of future career can you imagine for yourself? Short-term and/or long-term ...

Emma: I really like marketing and sales and at the moment I think I would like to stay in this area. To be honest, I don't know about long-term, but in the near future I would like to travel and learn more about the business and people.

Ms Williams: That fits well with our plans for you. We have realised that you seem to connect really well with customers and business partners and would like to offer you some intercultural training.

Emma: That sounds great. Do you think I should have some extra SAP training as well?

Ms Williams: Why don't we talk about this in a few months? The system often takes some time to get used to. Is there anything else you would like to do?

Emma: I would like to get more projects to supervise. And I have enrolled in a Spanish course, my personal target is to reach A2 level within the next year.

Ms Williams: I appreciate your motivation. If you achieve that, we can talk about the company paying for some one-to-one training with Ms Fernandez. Now, concerning the projects, I have talked to Ms Summers and she would like to assign you the task of handling the business cooperation with Event Concert.

Emma: I would like that very much.

Ms Williams: So, I hear you are playing in a band?

Emma: Yes, it's the best band ever. {...}

Aspect	Topic or points made
small talk	
work atmosphere	
positive feedback	
criticism or room for improvement	
general goals	
specific targets	

29 Fill in the exercise with the correct form of modal auxiliaries and the tense given. Use substitute forms when necessary.

can = "to be able to"/"to be allowed to"; may = "to be allowed to";
must = "to have to"; must not = "to not be allowed to"; need = "to have to"
should/shall/ought to = "to be supposed to"/"to be expected to";

1. Emma ______________________ do some intercultural training.
   (can or may, present simple)
2. Emma ______________________ worry about the performance review.
   (not, need, past simple)
3. Ms Williams ______________________ gather positive feedback.
   (can, present perfect)
4. Emma ______________________ play the guitar long before she moved to Munich.
   (can, past perfect).
5. The staff ______________________ smoke inside the building.
   (never, must not, present perfect)
6. Emma ______________________ take on more responsibility in a few years.
   (should, will-future)

Vocabulary

accomplishment	Leistung, Ausführung, Errungenschaft
to acquire	erwerben, beschaffen, erreichen
to adapt	an-/übernehmen
appraisal	Einschätzung
appraisal meeting	Mitarbeitergespräch
appraisal report	Gutachten, Bewertung
to assign	beauftragen, zuteilen

355694

to avoid	vermeiden
to be in charge of	verantwortlich sein
bullet point	Stichpunkt
to capitalise (UK), -ize (US)	groß schreiben
capitalisation (UK), capitalization (US)	Großschreibung
colon	Doppelpunkt
common	gewöhnlich, üblich
conduct	Verhalten, Benehmen
to confirm	bestätigen
consistent	einheitlich, gleichmäßig, konsequent
contribution	Beitrag
criticism	Kritik
curious	seltsam, eigenartig; auch neugierig
custom	Brauch
customary	üblich, gebräuchlich
to drain	abziehen, ablassen
to enrol	sich einschreiben
to expand	ausweiten, erweitern
flawless	makellos, ohne Fehler
formatting	Formatierung
to found, founded, founded	gründen
fragment	Fragment, Bruchstück
goal	Ziel, Tor
heading	Überschrift (über Paragraphen)
headline	Überschrift (über Artikel, z. B. Zeitung)
industry	Branche, Industrie
inexperience	Unerfahrenheit
to insult	beleidigen
intercultural	interkulturell
lettered	mit Buchstaben versehen
long-term	langfristig
lower case	klein geschrieben
to lure	locken
outstanding	herausragend
performance	Leistung
to point out	herausstellen, betonen, erwähnen
principal (Adj.)	Haupt-, hauptsächlich, wichtig
proximity	Nähe
punctuality	Pünktlichkeit
punctuation	Interpunktion, Satzzeichen
report	Bericht
reserve	Förmlichkeit, Reserviertheit
review	Bericht, Rückblick
to settle in	sich eingewöhnen
short-term	kurzfristig
to simplify	vereinfachen
stereotype	Stereotyp (Vorurteil)
style guide	Anleitung für Stil und Formatierung
subsidiary	Niederlassung
to supervise	betreuen, kontrollieren
target	Ziel, Zielscheibe
to vanish	verschwinden

C. Travelling Abroad

Emma is going on her first business trip. She is going to London for a fair and afterwards she is visiting a good customer of Blum Music. She is organising the trip and has to book a flight, a hotel and a rental car.

30 Emma books her flight to London online. Label the flight search engine with the German equivalents.

From ______________________

enter a country, city or airport

To ______________________

enter a country, city or airport

____

- Prefer directs ______________________
- return ______________________
- one way ______________________

Depart ______________________

05/05/201..

05/05/201..

Passengers ______________ 1 adults ______________ 0 children ______________ 0

Economy
Premium Economy
Business Class
First Class

____

Flight details: ______________________

- window seat ______________________
- aisle ______________________
- luggage ______________________
- 0 pieces ______________________
- vegetarian ______________________
- food allergies ______________________

____

search

31 Emma has already booked a room at The Kensington Close, but has not received any confirmation. Write her email using the words in the box.

concerning	*reservation*	*single room*	*non-smoker*	*three nights*
from 01/06 to 04/06	*received*	*confirmation*	*advance*	*regards*

From:	emmafrey@BlumMusic.com
To:	Info@KensingtonClose.uk
Subject:	Room reservation

Send

from/CC/BCC

Dear Sir or Madam,

____

____

____

____

____

____

____

____

____

____

Emma Frey

ole Play

32 Rent a car. Go to partner files on pages 113 and 116 and role play Emma's telephone call to the rental car company. Your call should include: opening, exchanging information, booking the car, closing. Remember to be polite.

Finally, June has arrived and Emma is on her way to London. Emma has travelled before, but never alone. She is both excited and nervous. People were full of good advice: Her mum told her what to pack. Nadine told her to leave some space in her suitcase to be able to bring back the things she will buy in London. Rebecca told her to not see the changing of the guards but rather go to one of the galleries which are all free. And Frankie told her to check out a comedy club in Soho where stand-up comedians try out their routines on Mondays.

33 Explain the steps of travelling by plane. Here are some words that might help:

Arrivals – Departures – Customs – Passport Control – Check in – Boarding Area – On Board – Security Check – Baggage Claim – Airport Shop – Information Desk

ole Play

34 Role play Emma's flight. Take turns being Emma, the airport staff and flight attendant. Check in – On Board (beverages and food etc.)

35 When you fly abroad or stay at a hotel, you often have to fill out a form. Label the form with their German equivalents in 35a and then fill out the form with your information in 35b.

35a **General Information (1):** ____________________

Title (2): ____________________

Family Name/Surname (3): ____________ First Name/Christian Name (4): ____________

Date of Birth (5): ____________ Gender (6): ____________

Marital status (7): ____________________

Single (8) Married (9) Divorced (10) Widow(er) (11) Separated (12) PACS (13)

____

____

Your current address and phone number (14): ____________________

Address (15): ____________ Passport number (23): ____________

City (16): ____________ Passport's country (24): ____________

Zip code/Postal code (17): ____________ Passport issuance date (25): ____________

Country (18): ____________ Passport expiry date (26): ____________

Phone number (19): ____________________

Cellphone/mobile number (20): ____________________

Country of birth (21): ____________________

Nationality (22): ____________________

35b **General Information**

Title: ____________________

Family Name: ____________ First Name: ____________

Date of Birth: ____________ Gender: ____________

Marital status: ____________________

Single Married Divorced Widow(er) Separated PACS

Your current address and phone number

Address: ____________ Passport number: ____________

City: ____________ Passport's country: ____________

Zip code/Postal code: ____________ Passport issuance date: ____________

Country: ____________ Passport expiry date: ____________

Phone number: ____________________

Cellphone/mobile number: ____________________

Country of birth: ____________________

Nationality: ____________________

355698

After Emma has landed at Stansted Airport, she takes the Stansted Express to get to London. She buys an Oyster Card with her train ticket – it is, after all, the cheapest and easiest way to use public transport in London. The London underground (or Tube) is simple to understand.

36 Emma arrives at Victoria Station and needs to go to High Street Kensington. Explain how she can get there. Remember that in the London underground stations it always says *Southbound, Northbound, Westbound* and *Eastbound*.

You can find the London tube map at http://www.bbc.co.uk/london/travel/downloads/tube_map.html.

37 With a partner, choose two places on the map and explain to each other how to get there.

Idea:
Research London sights in a travel guide or on the Internet. Find out which stations they are at and make a plan to see as many as possible in two days.

When Emma arrives at her hotel, she is already quite tired. She checks in and goes straight to her room. She immediately realises that it is a smoker room, but she is far too exhausted to do anything about it, so she doesn't fully unpack. The next morning she complains at the reception.

38 Match the sentence beginnings to the endings.

1. Excuse me, there seems
2. I had booked a non-smoker room, but I'm afraid
3. Would it be possible
4. Thank you, I would be
5. A cocktail on the house? That sounds
6. Thank you. I don't need help

a. to change rooms?
b. wonderful. Thank you.
c. moving my luggage.
d. to have been a misunderstanding.
e. it smells quite a bit like cigarettes in my room.
f. very grateful.

On her second evening, Emma meets Martin Jackson, the Eventline executive for dinner. He has invited her to a very nice pub called *The Anchor Inn* in Shoreditch. Although Emma has a map she is a bit lost and forgot where Martin said the pub was exactly. So she calls him on the phone.

Emma: Hi Martin. I am on my way but I think I am lost.

Martin: Do you know where you are?

Emma: I'm standing in front of this market building, I think it is Old Spitalfields Market, but I don't know which side.

Martin: What else do you see?

Emma: Well, there is an All Saints shop on the other side of the road.

Martin: Okay, then you are in Commercial Street, on the east side of the building. Turn left and go straight down Commercial Street in the direction of the Tube station "Shoreditch High Station".

Emma: Yes, I came from there. So I have to go back.

Martin: Yes, you do. You walked in the wrong direction. Commercial Street crosses Shoreditch High Street, you have to go half right and down that street for a few hundred meters. Once you arrived at the corner of the Tube station, don't turn right into Bethnal Street but continue down Commercial Street, and after a few meters turn right into Redchurch Street. *The Anchor Inn* is just before the junction with Club Row.

39 Draw a sketch of the way Emma has to go.

3556100

40 At the restaurant. Bring the conversation into the correct order.

__ **Emma:** Half a pint of cider, please.
__ **Bartender:** Sure.
__ **Emma:** Thanks a lot.
__ **Martin** (to Emma, after getting the drinks): Let's have a seat. Here is a menu.
__ **Emma:** Ooh, it all sounds great. I've realised that I love pub food. Anything particular you can recommend?
__ **Martin:** I'll go and order our food then.
__ **Emma:** Hello Martin. Thanks for the directions. It's so nice to see you. Thanks for inviting me.
__ **Martin** (to the bartender): Could we have half a pint of cider and a pint of ale, please?
__ **Emma:** It's really nice.
__ **Martin:** Yes, I love the Yorkshire pudding here, so maybe the mixed sausages with greens?
__ **Emma:** Sounds lovely. I'll have that.
__ **Martin:** I reserved a table in the back. We have to order at the bar, though. What would you like to drink?
__ **Martin:** Hello Emma. Glad, you found the place. I couldn't have you stay here in London without showing you my favourite pub.

41 Label the pictures

kale	*pork*	*pineapple*	*pear*	*poultry*	*turkey*
carrots	*beef*	*red currant*	*cherries*	*cucumber*	*potato*

Meat

(1) ____________

(2) ____________

(3) ____________

(4) ____________

Vegetable

(5) ____________

(6) ____________

(7) ____________

(8) ____________

Fruit

(9) ____________

(10) ____________

(11) ____________

(12) ____________

Idea:
In order to learn some more food English, why not try out English recipes?

After three days in London, Emma picks up her rental car to go to the little village in Rutland where the customer lives. Emma spent two days at the fair and one day visiting London sights. She only managed to see a very small part of London and has decided that she has to come back here soon. She also has done some extensive shopping since the exchange rate for the pound is very low and there are so many great shops in London. The company pays for expenses such as the flight and accommodation, and after almost a year of regular income, Emma thought it was about time to reward herself. She packs all her luggage and new acquisitions into her rental car and is on her way. The drive to the customer is not only a challenge because the British drive on the left, but also because some street signs are different, there are many roundabouts and there is a diversion.

42 Go to https://www.gov.uk/traffic-signs and look at the street signs. Do you understand all traffic signs? Explain two signs to your neighbour.

Label the signs here with their German meaning.

____

____

____

> Idea:
> Research currency and measurement converters on the Internet. Learn about UK and US measurements. How much is the euro worth today in dollars? How long is a mile? How tall are you in feet and inches? How much do you weigh in pounds?

The Participle, Gerund and Infinitive

Verben sind im Englischen besonders wichtig, viele Konstruktionen, z. B. mit Partizipien, werden dort verwendet, wo im Deutschen ein ganzer Nebensatz steht. Außer den Prädikatsformen (Verb + Zeit, Person) gibt es drei weitere Verbformen:

Form	Bildung	Verwendung
Gerund	Verb- ing	Das Verb als Nomen (im Deutschen das Verb mit Artikel und Großgeschrieben). e.g. I enjoy travelling./Ich mag das Reisen.
Infinitive	(to) Verb	Der Infinitiv ist die Grundform des Verbs. Meistens steht er in der Vewendung mit to, aber in manchen Verbindungen auch ohne. e.g. I advise you to call him./Ich rate Dir ihn anzurufen. He helped her carry the luggage./Er hat ihr geholfen, das Gepäck zu tragen.
Participle	Present: Verb- ing	Wird zur Bildung der progressive-Zeiten verwendet. Steht für Nebensätze. e.g. Walking down the street, I found a coin./Als ich die Straße hinabging, fand ich eine Münze. Das Verb als Adjektiv, mit aktiver Bedeutung. This is tiring./Das ist ermüdend. Entspricht der Deutschen -end-Endung.
Participle	Past: Verb -ed; 3rd Verb form	Wird zur Bildung der perfect-Zeiten und des Passivs verwendet. Steht für Nebensätze. e.g. The car stolen yesterday was found./Das Auto, das gestern gestohlen wurde, ist gefunden worden. Das Verb als Adjektiv, mit passiver Bedeutung. I feel beaten./Ich fühle mich geschlagen. Enstpricht dem Deutschen ge-Präfix.

Im Deutschen verwenden wir meistens den Infinitiv, um Verben anzuschließen. Das ist jedoch mehr eine Stilfrage als eine Grammatikregel. Im Englischen ist das anders, hier muss man wissen, welche Nomen und Adjektive von was gefolgt werden. Eine Regel ist, dass nach einer Präposition immer das Gerund steht.

Außerdem gibt es bei diesen Verben einen Bedeutungsunterschied, je nachdem was angeschlossen wird:

forget, remember, mean, stop, try, love, hate, prefer, like
e.g. Would you like to dance? → Möchtest Du (jetzt) tanzen?
Do you like dancing? → Tanzt Du gerne?

Attention!
Eine Liste findet sich z. B. hier: http://www.ego4u.de/de/cram-up/grammar/infinitive-gerund.

Emma really enjoyed her visit to Great Britain. Visiting the customer was very interesting and Emma was able to establish a good business relationship. As soon as she was home she realised she had brought another souvenir from England – a cold. She had to take a few days off and go on sick leave. Unfortunately, she also had to cancel band practice and that annoyed her for various reasons ... When she felt a little better and had stopped sniffling and coughing all the time, she sent a text message to Frankie to set up the next rehearsal. To her surprise, Frankie immediately called her and asked her if he could come over. Emma was very pleased.

43 Fill in the correct form of the verb: gerund, participle, infinitive (with or without to).

Emma: Hello Frankie. Thanks for ______________ (call). It's nice ______________ (see) you.

Frankie: I thought you could use some ______________ (cheer) up.

Emma: Indeed. Would you like something ______________ (drink)?

Frankie: Some coke, please. How did you like London? I loved ______________ (stay) there. ______________ (go) on the bus and just ______________ (look) at everything, I found it so much more diverse than Munich, if you know what I mean. And the clubs, they made me ______________ (dream of) ______________ (play) there one day. I loved it.

Emma: Me, too. I particularly enjoyed ______________ (walk) around and ______________ (get) to know the city a bit. But the time was so short, I didn't get the chance ______________ (see) much. I want ______________ (go) there again, soon. I know, when you are on a business trip it's not easy ______________ (get) in some sightseeing, but anyway, I love this job. The HR lady said that they are always glad ______________ (have) someone who does the ______________ (travel), since a lot of people have families ...

But how have you been? I was so mad that my cold meant ______________ (cancel) band practice. I miss it.

Frankie: Mhm ... Emma ... Listen ... With you ______________ (be) gone for a while, not ______________ (see) you for three weeks, it got me ______________ (think) ... I always look forward to ______________ (see) you so much, and I have tried ______________ (come up) with excuses ______________ (see) you ... So I thought ... Emma ... Would you like ______________ (go out) with me sometime? On a date?

Emma: I would love that. Absolutely.

3556104

Vocabulary

to abuse	missbrauchen
acquisitions	Errungenschaften
addiction	Abhängigkeit, Sucht
adult	Erwachsener
aggregate	gesamt, zusammengefasst
aisle	Gang
to annoy	nerven
arrival	Ankunft
to assert	behaupten, beanspruchen
baggage claim	Gepäckaufnahme
beans	Bohnen
beef	Rindfleisch
bell pepper	Paprika
berry	Beere
carrot	Karotte
to come over	vorbei kommen
communicable	übertragbar
concern	Bedenken, Sorge
confinement	hier: Haft; Beschränkung, Einengung
to convert	umrechnen
convicted	verurteilt
to cough	husten
currency	Währung
custody	Sorgerecht
customs	Zoll
to depart	abfahren, abfliegend, weggehen
departure	Abfahrt, Abflug
destination	Ziel
detained	inhaftiert
direct flight	Direktflug
direction	Richtung
disease	Krankheit
disorder	Störung
diverse	vielfältig, verschieden
diversion	Umleitung
to draw	zeichnen
espionage	Spionage
exchange rate	Wechselkurs
expenses	Auslagen (finanz.)
food allergy	Lebensmittelunverträglichkeit
fraud	Betrug
genocide	Völkermord
greens	Gemüsebeilage
immunity	Immunität
income	Einkommen
junction	Kreuzung
kale	Grünkohl
menu	Speisenkarte
peach	Pfirsich

pear	Birne
peas	Erbsen
persecution	Verfolgung
pineapple	Ananas
pomegranate	Granatapfel
pork	Schweinefleisch
poultry	Geflügel
prosecution	strafrechtliche Verfolgung
recipe	Kochrezept
to operate globally	weltweit handeln und operieren
to recommend	empfehlen
to remove	entfernen
rental car	Mietwagen
retained	einbehalten
return	Rückfahrt; -flug
to reward	belohnen
rhubarb	Rhabarber
roundabout	Kreisverkehr
sick leave	Krankheitsurlaub, Arbeitsunfähigkeit
sketch	Skizze
to sniffle	schniefen
stand-up comedian	Comedian, Kabarettist
text message	SMS
trafficker	Dealer, Händler
turkey	Truthahn
to turn right or left	links oder rechts abbiegen
turpitude	Schändlichkeit
veal	Kalb
violation	Verletzung

3556106

44 Crossword Puzzle

Across:

2 – the way things are done in a group or country
4 – to register in a course
6 – when a road is blocked you have to take this
9 – the kind of money used in a respective country
11 – three times
13 – before deductions
14 – if you do not do something on purpose
15 – transporting goods
16 – where you are going to

Down:

1 – a company has headquarters and this
3 – what you say if you are against something
5 – chicken, turkey and other meat from birds
7 – when you cannot go to work because you are ill
8 – suggestion
10 – after deductions
12 – proof

45 English in the Office – the Review Game

Roll the die. Choose one question or task from the number category you get. Every question or task should only be done once. Of course, once you've finished – you can always start over!

Spell your first and last name.
Describe your job
Talk about your routine.
Apologise for a colleague's absence.
Ask to change the date for a meeting.
Suggest where a visitor could spend the weekend.
Explain what to do at an airport when you are travelling.
Name the elements of an email.

Give your office number and mobile number.
A client tells you about a delay. React.
Name the elements of a CV.
Describe your favourite restaurant.
Ask for a list of prices and a brochure with the product range.
Welcome a visitor.
Explain how to get from your home to your work.
What qualities does someone need to do your job?

Give your complete office address.
Describe the room you are in.
What is the worst thing about your job?
A client has a bad headache. Help.
A customer complains about a quality issue. React.
Name the elements of a performance review.
Ask for a phone number and note it down.
Explain how the logistics department works.

Introduce yourself to a colleague.
What is the best thing about your job?
Describe a company regulation to a visitor.
Explain what the procurement department does.
Explain how to use local transport.
Describe a local dish to a foreign visitor.
Name some topics for good small talk.
Ask someone for assistance in an urgent project.

Say what your daily timetable is.
Describe the town you are from.
Ask someone to spell their name.
Explain what the sales department does.
Show disagreement. Politely.
Introduce one colleague to another.
Your visitor is unhappy with their hotel. Help.
Offer something to drink.

Describe yourself.
Ask for an email address and note it down.
Explain how a piece of equipment works.
Explain what the HR department does.
Accept an invitation to dinner.
Comment on the weather.
Suggest some places to go for dinner. Politely.
Explain the organisational structure of the company you work for.

3556108

Appendix

Grammar Basics

1. Adjectives and Adverbs

1.1 Adjectives	Adverbs
• nouns • link verbs: "to be", senses (sound, feel, taste, smell, look), other verbs that refer to the noun (see 1.4)	• verbs • adjectives • adverbs

1.2 Comparative/Superlative

Adjectives with one syllable: -er/-est
Adjectives with more the one syllable and Adverbs: more/most
All „wenig/weniger": less/least!
Comparative with "than"; the same: "as"/"as ... as"
Irregulars:
good/better/best; bad/worse/worst; ill/worse/worst;
much/more/most; many/more/most;
little/less/least
far/farther/farthest (local); far/further/furthest (all meanings)
near/nearer/nearest (in a district); near/nearer/next (in a line)
old/older/oldest (all meanings); old/elder/eldest (relatives or wisdom)

1.3 List of Irregular Adverbs

Adjective > adverb: good > well
keep their form: fast, hard, early, daily, straight;
only take form of adverb with a particular meaning:
high/highly; free/freely; late/lately; sharp/sharply;
difference in formality: wrong/wrongly; loud/loudly; near/nearly

1.4 List of Linking Verbs (which come with an Adjective)

act, appear, be, become, come, come out, end up, get, go, grow, feel, keep, look , prove, remain, seem, smell, sound, stay, taste, turn, turn up

2. Auxiliary Verbs

2.1 The Forms of "to be" Present and Past

Person	Singular	Plural
1st	I am; I was	we are; we were
2nd	you are; you were	you are; you were
3rd	he, she it is; he, she it was	they are; they were

2.2 Modal Auxiliaries

can, could, must, need, would, will, should, shall, ought to, might, may
→ always construct with an infinitive

Tenses: can = "to be able to"/"to be allowed to";
must = "to have to"; must not = "to not be allowed to"; may = "to be allowed to"; should/shall/ought to = "to be supposed to"/"to be expected to"; need = "to have to"

3. Conditionals

Pattern	Main Clause	If-Clause
0	present simple past simple	present simple past simple
1	will future/modal	present simple
2	would + Verb (Infinitive)	past simple
3	would have + Verb (3rd form)	past perfect

4. Verbs

4.1 Tenses (see *Tenses at One Glance*)

Progressive Tenses: always construct with "to be" + Verb-ing
Perfect Tenses: always construct with "to have" + Verb (3rd form)
A list of all irregular verbs can be found (to download) at:
http://www.ego4u.de/de/cram-up/grammar/irregular-verbs

List of non-progressive verbs:

Many of these verbs, such as feel and think, have a progressive form when they refer to an action rather than a state. Note that these verbs are often linking verbs which stand with an adjective, as they refer to a state and therefore the subject or noun.

appear
appreciate
be
believe
belong
care
consist of
contain
cost
dislike
doubt
envy
exist
fear
feel
hate
have
hear
imagine
include
know
like
look
love
mind
need
owe
own
possess
prefer
realise
recognise
remember
see
seem
smell
suppose
taste
think
think
understand
want
weigh

4.2 Passive

(see *Tenses at One Glance*) Always build with "to be" + Verb (3rd form); agent is connector "by".

4.3 Participles can stand as an adjective or to shorten a subclause!

Present Participle: Verb -ing → active meaning
dt: Verb -end (gehend)
Past Participle: Verb -ed → passive meaning
dt: ge-Verb (gegangen)

4.4 Infinitive (to do) vs. Gerund (doing)

Different meaning: hate, love, like, prefer; regret, forget, try, mean, stop, start.
Keep a list which words demand an infinitive with or without to, or a gerund.

5. Relative Clauses

who for people; which for things!
Differentiate between defining and non-defining relative clauses. Contact clause: the relative pronoun can be left out if it is an object in a defining relative clause.

3556110

6. Pronouns

Person	Singular			Plural
1.	I me my mine myself			we us our ours ourselves
2.	you you your yours yourself			you you your yours yourselves (!)
3.	**male** he him his his himself	**female** she her her hers herself	**neutral** (for all things!) it it its its itself	 they them their theirs themselves

Order: Subject
Object
Possessive (with noun following)
Possessive (no noun following)
Reflexive pronoun (oneself)

English Tenses At One Glance

Present Tense	
simple	**progressive/continuous**
Janet works at a bank. Verb (Infinitive), 3rd Ps/Sg + s Questions/Negatives: do/does (+ not)	Mr Smith is speaking on the phone. "to be" (am/is/are) + Verb -ing
Passive: I am called.	Passive: I am being called.
• facts that are permanently valid • repeated actions • schedules and timetables • basic tense in stories • verbs like: think, believe, depend etc.	• processes that are taking place at the moment of speaking or only for a certain amount of time • criticism • progress • near and certain future
KEY WORDS: always, every ..., never, often, seldom, sometimes, usually	at the moment, just, just now, listen!, look!, now, right now
Present Perfect	
simple	**progressive/continuous**
Have you heard the latest news? have/has + Verb -ed (3rd form/Past Participle)	We have been negotiating this deal for weeks. have/has been + Verb -ing
Passive: I have been called	– – –
• result/consequence is stressed • process has lasted a period of time up to the present • action that stopped recently	• see simple, plus: • speaker stresses the duration of the process (with time adverbial!) • stresses continuity
KEY WORDS: already, ever, just, never, not yet, so far, till/up to now	all day, for 4 years, since 1993, how long?, the whole week

Past Tense	
simple	**progressive/continuous**
Did you have a nice trip? Verb-ed (2nd form) Questions/Negatives: did (+ not)	John was finishing work when he received a call. "to be" (was/were) + Verb -ing
Passive: I was called.	Passive: I was being called.
• past actions or states that are over now • chain of actions • narrative tense (in stories)	• action that was in progress at a particular moment in the past • description of background events (in stories)
KEY WORDS: yesterday, ago, in 1990, the other day, last *, when/what time?	when, while, as long as

Past Perfect	
simple	**progressive/continuous**
We didn't have to wait since Ms Clay had booked tickets in advance. had + Verb -ed (3rd form/Past Part.)	It became clear that the product we had been testing would not work. had been + Verb -ing
Passive: I had been called.	– – –
• an event or state came before some other event or state in the past • an event or state had begun before a point in the past time and continued up to this point	• see simple, plus: • speaker stresses the duration of the process (with time adverbial!) • action was still in progress
KEY WORDS: already, ever, just, never, not yet, so far, till now, up to now	all day, for 4 years, since 1993, how long?, the whole week

Will-Future	
simple	**progressive/continuous**
The fair will end tomorrow. will + Infinitive	This time next year I will be travelling through the USA. will be + Verb -ing
Passive: I will be called.	– – –
• process in the future that cannot be influenced • action or state that is assumed to become true • spontaneous decision • promises/offers • after particular verbs: hope, expect, trust	• process that will be going on in the future (duration!)
KEY WORDS: assumption: I think, probably, we might ..., perhaps	

Going to-Future	
simple	**past going to (!)**
I am going to travel to the USA "to be" (am/are/is) going to + Verb (Inf)	I was going to visit the USA, but then I got sick. "to be" (was/were) going to + Verb (Inf)
Passive: – – –	– – –
personal plans for the future • decision and conclusion made for the future (based on present evidence)	• personal plans one had in the past, but didn't see through

Future Perfect (Future-in-the-Past)	
simple	**progressive/continuous**
I will have managed to do this by next week! will have + Verb -ed (3rd form/Pa. Part.)	This time tomorrow he will have been speaking for two hours. will be + Verb -ing
Passive: I will have been called.	– – –
• process that will have finished at a certain point in the future	• process that will have been going on for a certain time period in the future
KEY WORDS: by Monday, in a week	for ..., the last couple of *, all * long

Partner Files Student A

See page 27, Exercise 13

elephone
ole Plays

The information here sets up the situation. Your partner has the corresponding information. Read first what your role is. As the one receiving the call you will not understand everything immediately.
Then make the call. Make sure to stay polite and get all the information you need (e.g. spelling a name). If you want to make it more realistic, why don't you sit back to back?

1 **Caller:** Margaret Wilson, procurement
You call: OfficeStuff, a supplier
Purpose: Complaint. Three of the office chairs are not the same quality as the test chair. You want to return them.

2 Receive the call:
You are: George Lindner, Blum Music
Reaction: That's a problem. Urgently needed. You need a fixed date. If production stops they have to give discount of 15 %.

3 **Caller:** Tony, graphic designer
You call: Nadine Summers, Blum Music
Purpose: Discuss the visuals for the brochure. Picture format is not good, need higher definition. Also reconsider choice of picture. Too conservative.

4 Receive the call:
You are: Hiley Music Shop, a retailer.
Reaction: You want to do this. Next week is closed. The week after next week on Thursday only between ten and two.

5 **Caller:** Meredith Williams
You call: Work for the Day, a time work agency
Purpose: You need some extra short-term workers for the inventory. Two, must be reliable and concentrated in their work. Three Saturdays in January.

6 Receive the call:
You are: John Miller
Reaction: George Lindner is out of office. Offer to take a message. Note everything down.

See page 94, Exercise 32

ole Play

Emma calls the rental agency. Here is what she wants:
- rent a car;
- from 04/06 to 07/06;
- pick up in West London; return at Stansted Airport

See page 78, Exercise 16

Graph description

1.

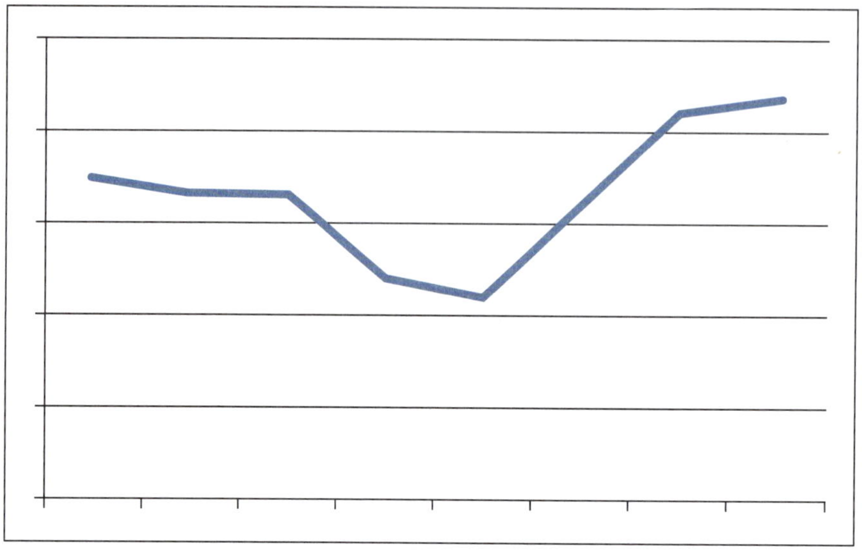

2.

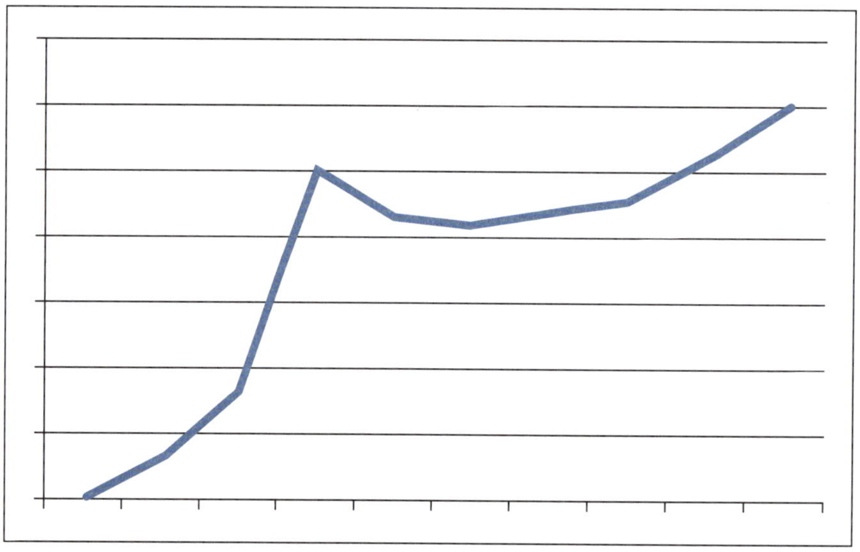

3.

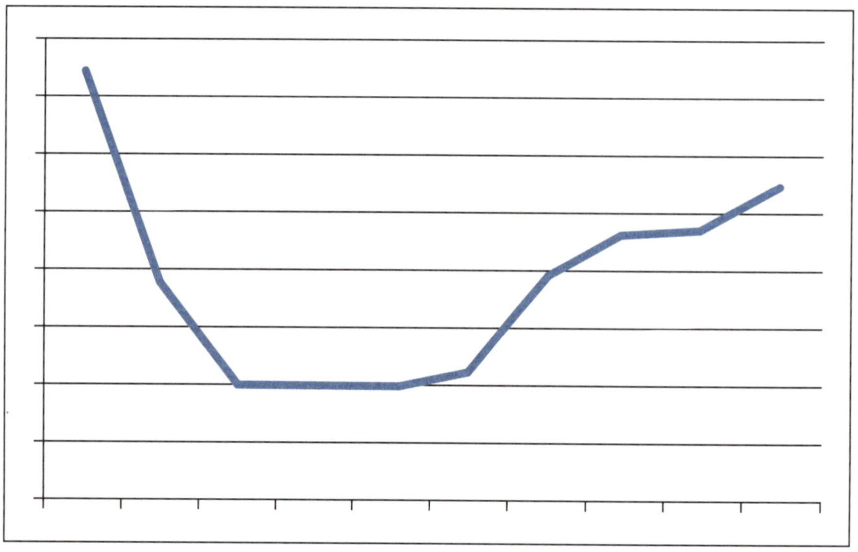

3556114

See page 59, Exercise 33

Here are some ideas for replacing the impolite phrases given. The sentences are not in the correct order. Match them to the right sentences.

Find out what the customer wants

What seems to be the problem?
How can I help you?
If I understand you correctly ... .
Could you rephrase that, please?
Could you repeat that, please?

Show understanding

Would it help if I ...?
I understand how you could feel this way.
We take customer complaints very seriously.
I see.
Of course, this is an issue we should deal with.

Find out details

Let me just read this back to you.
Could you please tell me the delivery number?
Could you tell me when exactly you placed the order?
Is it possible to send me a copy of the invoice?
Please hold on for a minute. I'll look into this.

Offer assistance

I'm afraid we cannot take care of this, but calling xy might be an idea.
I will take care of this personally.
We are working on this problem.
I'm afraid I cannot help you with this, but I will put you through to the quality department.

Close the call

You are welcome.
Is there anything else I can help you with?
Have a good day. Goodbye.
If anything else comes up, please don't hesitate to contact us.

Partner Files Student B

See page 27, Exercise 13

Telephone Role Plays

The information here sets up the situation. Your partner has the corresponding information. Read first what your role is. As the one receiving the call you will not understand everything immediately.
Then make the call. Make sure to stay polite and get all the information you need (e.g. spelling a name). If you want to make it more realistic, why don't you sit back to back?

1 Receive the call:
You are: OfficeStuff, supplier for office furniture
Reaction: Alternative chairs? Delivery costs stay with Blum Music. You are not happy.

2 **Caller:** Ted Baker
You call: George Lindner, Blum Music
Purpose: The order for strings No 2924840-33 is delayed. Arrival two days later than planned. Apologise. Reason for delay: Truck broke down in the middle of nowhere in the US.

3 Receive the call:
You are: Nadine Summers
Reaction: Different format is no problem. New pictures are planned, but for now that's all you have.

4 **Caller:** Sean Edson
You call: Hiley Music Shop, a retailer
Purpose: You want to set up a meeting to present the new guitar. Anytime next week is fine. Week after next week, only Thursday.

5 Receive the call:
You are: Work for the Day, a time work agency
Reaction: No problem. What do you need exactly? When?

6 **Caller:** Zoya Sidhwani
You call: George Lindner, Blum Music
Purpose: You want to discuss an order. Leave a message. Please call back.
Your number 0091-555-832 998

See page 94, Exercise 32

Role Play

Receive the call as the rental car company. Here is what you need to know and say:
- the car is needed when and where, how long, where exactly in London?
- costs are € 270; full comprehensive insurance is included.

3556116

See page 78, Exercise 16

Graph description

1.

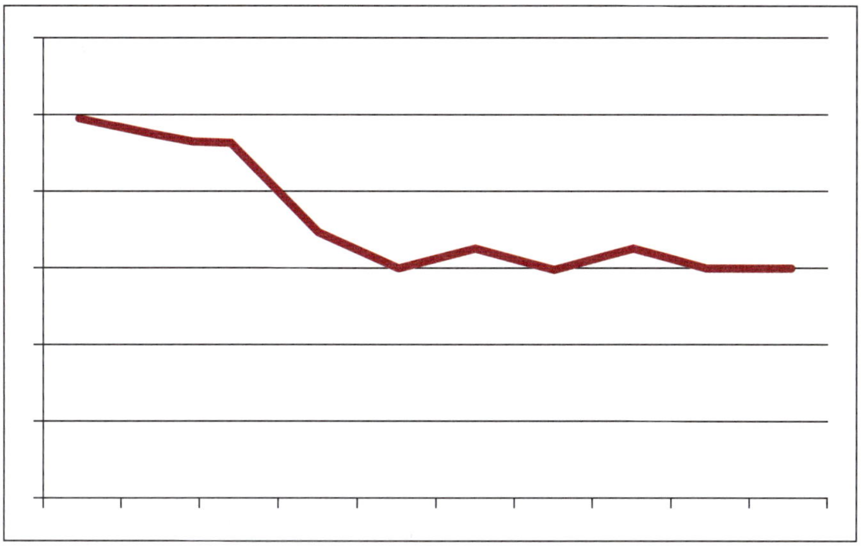

2.

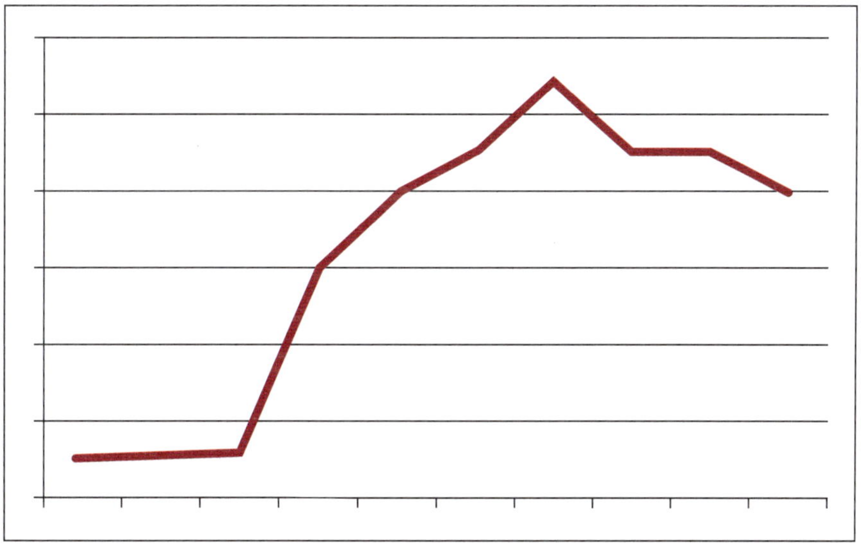

3.

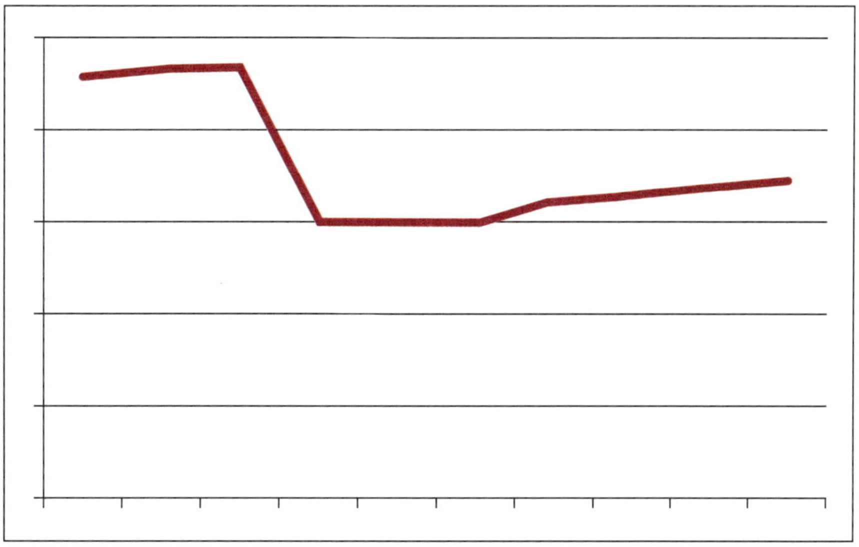

Dealing with a Visitor – a Walk-Through

See page 34, Exercise 2

Reception

Good morning. Good afternoon. Good evening. How are you?
Nice to meet you.

How was your trip?
Thanks, fine. Everything went well.
There were some problems with ... My flight was delayed. There was a lot of traffic, but I managed to get here on time.
The next time, you could come here by train. Yes, the streets are really full/overcrowded.

Is your hotel okay? Is the accommodation fine?
Did you have any breakfast? Was the breakfast all right?

Before the meeting

Please follow me to my office/our meeting room. Please have a seat.
Would you like a cup of coffee/any refreshments/any beverages/anything to drink?

Here you are.
Thank you.
You're welcome. Welcome. Not at all.
So, shall we talk business now?

> Attention!
> Wie in vielen Sprachen heißt im Englischen *Bitte* beim Überreichen nicht *Please* sondern *Here you are* und als Erwiderung auf ein Danke *You're welcome.*

Having a break

Would you like to have lunch now?
Shall we go for lunch?
Let's have a break and have a short lunch.
Let's have a lunch break.
Are you a smoker or non-smoker? Here is the smoking area. I'll fetch some coffee for us ...

At lunch

Enjoy your meal. Enjoy!

Topics for conversation:
- Market – Industry – Business – Economy: Have you heard ...?
- Cultural anecdotes: history – typical habits – special food
- Weather
- Hobbies
- Sports
- News

I'm afraid we have to leave now.
I think we should go back to the meeting room.
Is everyone finished/done?

Saying goodbye

It was nice meeting you.
Thank you for your visit. Thanks for having me (AE). Thank you for the invitation.

I wish you a good trip back.
See you tomorrow.
Have a nice evening. Same to you.

Phrases for Argumentation

See page 75

Agreeing

I have the same opinion. I am of the same opinion.
I agree. I completely agree.
Agreed.
Okay.
That's a good idea.
Yes, you are right.
I think so, too. (Das finde ich auch.)
I don't think so, either. (Das finde ich auch nicht.)

Suggesting

How about (doing sth.) ...? How about looking at the project again?
Why not ...? Why don't we ...?
It's just an idea, but why don't you ...?
Maybe you could ...?
I think the best would be to do sth.
Shall we ...? Should we ...?
Let's try doing ...
What do you think about ...?

Negotiation

For us it's essential to know ...
Our priority is ...
I'm afraid this is not possible for us ...
It's a question of ...
One thing we need to discuss ...
Could you please explain to me how ...
One thing I don't quite understand here ...
Have you thought about ...?
You need to be aware of ...
If you (present simple), we will (infinitve)
If you (past simple), we would (infinitive)
I think sth. should be done ...
If we can agree on this, let's move on to the next point.
I understand your position, ...

This is what we can offer: ...
We can accept these conditions, if ... (present simple)
Okay, we can compromise here ...
I would like to make the following suggestion ...

This is clearly an (dis-) advantage for both parties.
I can fully agree with you on this.

We are looking forward to doing business with you.

Disagreeing

I'm afraid I don't agree. I don't fully/really agree.
I don't think so.
That might not be such a good idea.
I think that's not such a good idea.
I'm afraid that ...
Yes, but ... I see your point, but ...
Although I understand what you are saying, I think ...
... we have to consider ...; we haven't thought about ...; (we = referring to the two people in the conversation)
... you have to consider ...; ... please don't forget that ...;
Ask open questions to show your doubt.

Give reasons/argumentation

It would be of advantage to do ...
A great advantage of this is ...
The benefit of this is .../The disadvantage of this would be ...
This is clearly an opportunity to do ...
The most important thing to consider is ...

Language of Presentations

See page 87

Introduction

Can everyone see? Well, good morning ladies and gentlemen. Thank you for coming.
Before we start I'd like to introduce myself.
I know I've met some of you, but just for the benefit of those I haven't, my name's ...

I'm here to	talk about
I'm going to	present
I'd like to	explain
	brief you on
	inform you about
	describe

The subject/focus/topic of my presentation is ...
The purpose of this talk is to ...
I'd like to begin with (doing) ...

Linking and orientation

first of all – secondly – then – after that – finally
regarding – concerning – in respect to
moreover – furthermore – in addition
on the other hand – however – nonetheless
in spite of – despite – although
summarising – to sum up – all in all

I've divided my presentation into three main parts ...
As I've mentioned earlier ...

Questions

I'd be glad to answer any questions at the end of my talk.
If you have any questions, please feel free to interrupt.
Any questions so far?

Visuals

I'd like (you) to look at ...
You will see that ...
The figures/graph shows/demonstrates/illustrates that ...

Statements (strong)

I would like to claim/state/maintain ...
I must emphasise that ...

Conclusion

In conclusion, let me briefly go through the main points again.
Right, I think that's everything. Let me finish by thanking you for your attention.
All in all, I think we can conclude that ...

3556120

Vocabulary – Alphabetical Order

This list entails some additional vocabulary. The IPA (International Phonetical Alphabet) is not provided here, but you can listen how to pronounce words on the Internet, e.g. at www.leo.org or www.dict.cc.

a	
abbreviate	abkürzen
abroad	im Ausland
abuse	missbrauchen
accessory	Accessoire, Zubehör
accommodation	Unterbringung, Unterkunft
accompany	begleiten
accomplishment	Leistung, Ausführung, Errungenschaft
account	Bericht, Konto, Kundenauftrag
accounting	Zahlungswesen, Finanzabteilung, Buchhaltung
accustomed	gewohnt
achieve	erreichen
acquire	erwerben, beschaffen, erreichen
acquisitions	Errungenschaften, Einkäufe
ad, advert, advertisement	(Werbe-) Anzeige
adapt	an-/übernehmen
add	addieren
addiction	Abhängigkeit, Sucht
additionally	zusätzlich
administrative	Verwaltungs-
adult	Erwachsener
advantage	Vorteil
advise	raten, anweisen
agenda	Tagesordnung, Plan, Absicht
aggregate	gesamt, zusammengefasst
agree	zustimmen
agreement	Übereinkunft, Zustimmung
air vent	Belüfter, Ventilator
aisle	Gang
all in all	alles in allem
ambitious	ehrgeizig
amount	Menge, Betrag
amount due	fälliger Betrag
ample	ausreichend
announce	ankündigen
annoy	nerven, aufregen
answer to so.	jmd. Rechenschaft ablegen, hier: jmd. untergeben sein
appealing	ansprechend
application	Anwendung
apply for	sich bewerben um
appointment	Termin
appraisal	Einschätzung
appraisal meeting	Mitarbeitergespräch
appraisal report	Gutachten, Bewertung

appreciate	schätzen, würdigen
apprenticeship	Ausbildung, Lehre
appropriate	passend
approval	Zustimmung
arrival	Ankunft
as follows	wie folgt
assert	behaupten, beanspruchen
assign	beauftragen, zuteilen
assignment	Aufgabe
assist	helfen
associate	verbinden mit
assume	annehmen
assure	sicherstellen, versichern
attach	anhängen
attached	im Anhang
attachment	Anhang
avoid	vermeiden

b

baggage claim	Gepäckaufnahme
ballpoint pen	Kugelschreiber
bar chart	Säulendiagramm
be firm	fest stehen, fix sein
be in charge of	verantwortlich sein
be off	eigenartig sein
be responsible for	verantwortlich sein für
be supposed to	sollen
beans	Bohnen
beef	Rindfleisch
bell pepper	Paprika
benefit	Vorteil
berry	Beere
beverages	Getränke
bill of delivery	Lieferschein
bill of lading	Lieferschein
binding	bindend
biweekly	vierzehntägig
bold	fett (gedruckt)
bookkeeping	Buchhaltung
booth	Stand, Zelle
brainstorm	Ideen sammeln
brand	Marke
break sth. in	(Schuhe) einlaufen, (Kleidung) eintragen, etc.
breathtaking	atemberaubend
brochure	Prospekt, Broschüre
brush up	aufbessern
buffer stock	Pufferbestand
bullet point	Stichpunkt
busy	beschäftigt, hier: besetzt
button	Knopf
buy	kaufen

buyer	Käufer
c	
cabinet	Schrank
calculate	berechnen, kalkulieren
capital letter	Großbuchstabe
capitalisation (UK), capitalization	Großschreibung
capitalise (UK), -ize (US)	groß schreiben
cargo	Fracht
carpet	Teppich
carrier	Transportunternehmen
carrot	Karotte
cell (phone), mobile phone	Handy
chair	vorsitzen
chamber of commerce	Handelskammer
character	Schriftzeichen
charge (verb)	berechnen (Kosten)
charges	Kosten, Gebühren
check	überprüfen
cheerful	fröhlich
clause	Klausel
clockwise	im Uhrzeigersinn
coffee maker	Kaffeemaschine
colon	Doppelpunkt
come over	vorbei kommen
come up with	sich einfallen lassen
commence	beginnen
commodity	Handelsware
common	gewöhnlich, üblich
communicable	übertragbar
company	Firma
competition	Wettbewerb, Mitbewerber
competitive	ehrgeizig, hier: wettbewerbsfähig
complain	sich beschweren
complaint	Beschwerde
complement	Zubehör
complete	vervollständigen, ergänzen
comply to (regulations)	einhalten (Regeln)
comprise	umfassen, beinhalten
concern (noun)	Sorge, Betreff, Bedenken
concern (verb)	betreffen
concerning	betreffend
condition	Bedingung, Zustand
conduct	Verhalten, Benehmen
confident	zuversichtlich, selbstbewusst
confinement	hier: Haft; Beschränkung, Einengung
confirm	bestätigen
confirmation	Bestätigung
consensus	Konsens, Übereinstimmung
consent	Abmachung, Übereinkunft
consider	bedenken, einschätzen, in Erwägung ziehen

considerable	bemerkenswert
consideration	Erwägung, Betrachtung; hier: Entgelt, Gegenleistung
consignee	Warenempfänger
consistent	einheitlich, gleichmäßig, konsequent
consolidate	konsolidieren, zusammenfassen
consumables	Verbrauchsgüter
content	Inhalt
continuous improvement – also: lean management or Kaizen	kontinuierlicher Verbesserungs-prozess
contract	Vertrag
contribution	Beitrag
convert	umrechnen
convicted	verurteilt
copying machine	Kopierer
corporate	Firmen-
corporate identity	einheitliche Gestaltung eine Firma betreffend
correspond	korrespondieren, sich schreiben
cost-efficiency	Kosteneffizienz, Kosteneinsparung
cough	husten
counter-clockwise	gegen den Uhrzeigersinn
court	Gericht
cover	abdecken
crane	Kran
criticism	Kritik
cross check	überprüfen (im Vergleich)
curious	seltsam, eigenartig; auch neugierig
currency	Währung
current	aktuell
curriculum	Lehrplan, Kursplan
curtain	Vorhang
custody	Sorgerecht
custom	Brauch
customary	üblich, gebräuchlich
customer	Kunde
customised (UK), -ized (US)	auf den Kunden zugeschnitten
customs	Zoll

d

debits	Schulden
decoration	Dekoration
deduction	Abzug
delay	Verspätung
deliberate	bewusst, absichtlich
delivery	Lieferung
delivery slip	Lieferschein
delivery ticket	Lieferschein
demand	Nachfrage
depart	abfahren, abfliegend, weggehen
departure	Abfahrt, Abflug

desire	wünschen, ersehnen
desk	Schreibtisch
despite	trotz
destination	Ziel
detained	inhaftiert
direct flight	Direktflug
direction	Richtung
directions	Wegbeschreibung
disadvantage	Nachteil
disagree	ablehnen, nicht zustimmen
discount	Rabatt
disease	Krankheit
disorder	Störung
dispatch	absenden
distribution chain	Lieferkette (Verteilung)
diverse	vielfältig, verschieden
diversify	sich breiter aufstellen, erweitern
diversion	Umleitung
divide	teilen
draft	Entwurf
drain	abziehen, ablassen
draw	zeichnen
drawing	Zeichnung
due to (plus noun)	wegen
duty	Pflicht
e	
e.g.	z. B. (zum Beispiel)
economy	Wirtschaft
efficiency	Wirksamkeit, Effizienz
effortless	anstrengungslos, unangestrengt
employee	Angestellte(r), Arbeitnehmer
employer	Arbeitgeber
enclose	beifügen
enclosure	Anlage
end user	Endverbraucher
energetic	energiegeladen
energy consumption	Energieverbrauch
enforceable	vollziehbar, einklagbar
engage	miteinbeziehen, anheuern, verpflichten
engagement	Verbindlichkeit, Verpflichtung
enquiry (UK), inquiry (US)	Anfrage, Angebotsanfrage
enrol	sich einschreiben
ensure, to make sure	sicherstellen
enter	eingeben
equals	ist gleich
equipment	Ausstattung, Ausrüstung
espionage	Spionage
estimate	schätzen (eine Zahl)
evidence	belegen, beweisen
ex works	ab Werk

Excel sheet	Excel Tabelle
exchange rate	Wechselkurs
excuse	hier: Ausrede
executive	Manager (leitend)
exhibition	Ausstellung
expand	ausweiten, erweitern
expansion	Erweiterung, Ausbau
expenses	Auslagen (finanz.)
exporter	Exporteur
extent	Ausmaß
f	
fabric	Stoff
facility	Einrichtung
factory	Fabrik
fair	gerecht
faithfully	hochachtungsvoll
famous	berühmt
far, further, furthest	weit, weiter(e), am weitesten
fee	Gebühr
fetch	holen
figures	Zahlen, Wert
file (noun)	Akte
file (verb)	ablegen
first-name basis (to be on a)	beim Vornamen (sich nennen)
fitting	passend
flawless	makellos, ohne Fehler
folder	Ordner
font	Schrift
food allergy	Lebensmittelunverträglichkeit
forecast	Vorhersicht, Vorausschau
fork lift	Gabelstapler
formatting	Formatierung
forwarding agency	Spedition
found, founded, founded	gründen
fragile	zerbrechlich
fragment	Fragment, Bruchstück
franco domicile	frei Haus
frank	ehrlich
fraud	Betrug
freelance	selbständig
freight	Fracht
fringe benefit	(vertragliche) Nebenleistungen
full comprehensive insurance	Vollkasko
g	
gathering	Zusammenkunft
general terms and conditions	Allgemeine Geschäftsbedingungen (AGBs)
genocide	Völkermord
goal	Ziel, Tor
good	Ware
goods issue	Warenausgang

3556126

goods receipt	Wareneingang
graph chart	Graph, Liniendiagramm
greens	Gemüsebeilage
gross	brutto
h	
handle	bearbeiten, erledigen
handsome	gutaussehend
hang out	Zeit verbringen
hazardous	gefährlich
heading	Überschrift (über Paragraphen)
headline	Überschrift (über Artikel, z. B. Zeitung)
headset	Kopfhörer mit Sprechfunktion
hesitate	zögern
high-end	hochwertig, teuer
hike	wandern
hole puncher	Locher
horrid	schrecklich
household chores	Aufgaben im Haushalt
however	jedoch
HR (human resources department)	Personalwesen
hug	Umarmung
hyphen	Bindestrich
i	
i. e.	d. h. (das heißt)
I'm afraid	Ich befürchte
immunity	Immunität
impeccable	perfekt, makellos
imply	implizieren
importer	Importeur
impressed	beeindruckt
impression	Eindruck
improve	verbessern
in advance	im Voraus
indicate	andeuten
in reference to	in Bezug auf
in regard to	In Bezug auf, bezogen auf
in respect to	In Bezug auf, bezogen auf
in spite of	trotz
in turns	abwechselnd
in-house	in der Firma, intern
income	Einkommen
incoming	herein kommend
Independence Day	Unabhängigkeitstag
indicate	andeuten
industry	Branche, Industrie
inequitable	unbillig (ungerecht)
inexperience	Unerfahrenheit
initial	beginnend
inquire	fragen, nachfragen
instalment plan	Zahlungsplan

instructor	Lehrer, Anleiter
insufficient	unzureichend
insult	beleidigen
insurance policy	Versicherungspolice
intercultural	interkulturell
interest rate	Zinsen
intern	PraktikantIn
internship	Praktikum
interrupt	unterbrechen
investment	Investition
invoice	Rechnung
involve	miteinbeziehen, hier: beinhalten
italics	kursiv
item number	Artikelnummer
itinerary	Reiseplan
j	
job interview	Vorstellungsgespräch
junction	Kreuzung
just in time	Just-in-Time System (Anlieferung kurz vor Zeitpunkt der Verarbeitung)
Just kidding.	Nur Spaß
k	
kale	Grünkohl
l	
label (noun)	Kennzeichnung, Musiklabel
label (verb)	kennzeichnen
laid-back	entspannt
laminate floor	Laminat
lane	Gang
launch	auf den Markt bringen, in Gang setzen
lead time	Durchlaufzeit, Vorlaufzeit, Vorhaltezeit
lease	verleihen, leasen
legal	rechtlich
lettered	mit Buchstaben versehen
letterhead	Briefkopf
liberty	Freiheit
line graph	Liniendiagramm
link	Verbindung
literate	belesen, fähig
load	laden, verladen
loading dock	Ladedock
logo	Firmenlogo
long-term	langfristig
look forward to doing something	sich darauf freuen etwas zu tun
look forward to something	sich auf etwas freuen
lower case	klein geschrieben
lure	locken
lyrics	Liedtext

3556128

m	
maintain	aufrecht erhalten, behaupten
man-hours	Arbeitsstunden
manufacturer	Hersteller
map	Karte
market	Markt
marketing	Marketing
masterpiece	Meisterwerk
matter of taste	Geschmackssache
means	Mittel
meeting	Besprechung
menu	Speisenkarte
minutes	Protokoll
monitor	überwachen, beaufsichtigen
mouse	Maus, Mouse
mouse pad	Mousepad
muffle (sound)	dämpfen (Lärm)
multiply	multiplizieren
mutual	gegenseitig
n	
negotiation	Verhandlung
net	netto
night shift	Nachtschicht
o	
objection	Einwand
obvious	offensichtlich
occasional	gelegentlich
occupation	Beruf
offer	Angebot
office	Büro
on call order	Bestellung auf Abruf
one-to-one training	Einzeltraining
operating globally	weltweit handeln, operieren
opportunity	Gelegenheit, Möglichkeit
order	Bestellung
order number	Bestellnummer, Artikelnummer
organisational chart	Organigramm
ornaments	Schmuck
outsource	auslagern
outstanding	herausragend, ausstehend
own	besitzen
owner	Eigentümer, Besitzer
p	
packing list	Lieferschein, Packliste
page-turner	Schmöker, sehr spannendes Buch (bei dem man schnell die Seiten umblättert)
pallet	Palette
pallet rack	Gestell für Paletten
pants	Hosen (US)

particular	besonders
particularly	besonders
party	Partei
peach	Pfirsich
peak	Spitze
pear	Birne
peas	Erbsen
performance	Leistung
persecution	Verfolgung
personal	persönlich, privat
personnel	Personal-
phrase	formulieren
pick	wählen, auswählen, aussuchen
pick-by-...	Kommissionierung durch ...
pie chart	Tortendiagramm
pillow	Kissen
pineapple	Ananas
piping	Rohrleitungen
plummet	ins Bodenlose fallen, abstürzen
point out	herausstellen, betonen, erwähnen
pomegranate	Granatapfel
pork	Schweinefleisch
poultry	Geflügel
preference	Vorliebe
principal (Adj.)	Haupt-, hauptsächlich, wichtig
printer	Drucker
process	bearbeiten, verarbeiten
procurement	Beschaffung
profit	Profit, Gewinn
promotion	Werbeaktion, Beförderung
promotional	Werbe-
proof-read	Korrektur lesen
proposal	Vorschlag
propose	vorschlagen
prosecution	strafrechtliche Verfolgung
protect	schützen
proximity	Nähe
public holiday	Feiertag
publication	Veröffentlichung
punctuality	Pünktlichkeit
punctuation	Interpunktion, Satzzeichen
purchase	Einkauf
quadruple	vierfach
query	Frage, Anfrage
quite	ziemlich
quotation	Kostenvoranschlag
r	
rapid	schnell
re-order level	Bestand sollte mit Nachbestellung aufgefüllt werden.

3556130

read back	wiederholen
receipt	Quittung
receipt of invoice	Erhalten der Rechnung
receive	empfangen
recent	kürzlich, vor kurzem
recently	kürzlich
reception	Empfang
recipe	Kochrezept
recommend	empfehlen
refreshments	Erfrischungen
regards	Grüße
regret	bedauern
rehearse	proben
remark	Anmerkung
reminder	Mahnung
remove	entfernen
rental car	Mietwagen
repeat order	Nachbestellung
report	Bericht
request	um etwas bitten, verlangen
requirement	Anforderung
reserve	Förmlichkeit, Reserviertheit
resolve	lösen, (Konto) ausgleichen
responsibility	Verantwortung, Aufgabenbereich
restriction	Einschränkung
retailer	Verkäufer (Laden)
retained	einbehalten
retrieval system	Abfragesystem
return	Rückfahrt; -flug
revenue	Umsatz
review	Bericht, Rückblick
revise	überarbeiten
reward	belohnen
rhubarb	Rhabarber
rocket	in die Höhe schießen, abheben
rough copy	Entwurf
roundabout	Kreisverkehr
s	
salary	Einkommen
sales representative	Vertriebsperson
sample	Sample, Beispielstück, Teststück
scanner	Scanner
seating surface	Sitzfläche
sell	verkaufen
seller	Verkäufer
service	Dienstleistung
set up	einrichten, festsetzen, aufbauen
settle	ausgleichen, begleichen
settle in	sich eingewöhnen
sew (spoken sow)	nähen

share	Aktie
sheet music	Noten
shipment	Transport
shipper	Verlader
shipping	Transport, Versand
short-term	kurzfristig
sick leave	Krankheitsurlaub, Arbeitsunfähigkeit
significant	bedeutend
similar	ähnlich
simplify	vereinfachen
sincere	aufrichtig
size	Größe
sketch	Skizze
skill	Fähigkeit
slash	Schrägstrich
sloppy	schlampig
smart	klug, gescheit
sniffle	schniefen
sociable	kontaktfreudig, gesellig, umgänglich
sort pocket	Ablagefach
space	Leerzeichen
spare part	Ersatzteil
square	Quadrat
staff	Mitarbeiter
stand	Messestand
stand-up comedian	Comedian, Kabarettist
standing order	Dauerauftrag, Abonnement
stapler	Tacker
stationery	Bürobedarf, Büromaterial
stereotype	Stereotyp (Vorurteil)
stipulated	festgelegt (vertraglich)
stock	Lager, Aktie
stock level	Bestand
storage	Lager
style guide	Anleitung für Stil und Formatierung
subject	Betreff
subscribe	abonnieren
subsidiary	Niederlassung
substitute	Ersatz
subtotal	Zwischensumme
subtract	subtrahieren
success	Erfolg
suggestion	Vorschlag
suitable	passend
supervise	betreuen, kontrollieren
supervisor	Vorgesetzter, Vorarbeiter
supplier	Zulieferer
supply	Angebot, Lieferung
supply chain	Lieferkette (Belieferung)
support	unterstützen
swap body	Wechselaufbau, Wechselbehälter

3556132

t	
table	Tabelle
tackle	behandeln, sich kümmern um (ein Thema)
talkative	gesprächig, redselig
target	Ziel, Zielscheibe
task	Aufgabe
tax	Steuer
tenancy	Pacht
terms of delivery	Lieferbedingungen
terms of payment	Zahlungsbedingungen
text message	SMS
the latter	letzteres
therefore	somit
time frame	Zeitrahmen
time slot	Zeitraum (im Kalender)
time-critical	dringend
to adapt to	sich anpassen
to smirk	grinsen
to soar	fliegen
toolbar	Menü
total	gesamt ausmachen
total	Summe
toxic	giftig
trace	verfolgen (Spur)
trade fair	Messe
trafficker	Dealer, Händler
training on the job	Lernen im Job
tremendous	enorm, sehr viel
trial order	Probebestellung
trip	Reise
triple	dreifach
turkey	Truthahn
turn right or left	links oder rechts abbiegen
turpitude	Schändlichkeit
type up	zusammenschreiben
u	
underline/underscore	unterstreichen
underpants	Unterhosen
unfortunately	leider
unload	ausladen, abladen
urgent	dringend
urgent	dringend
v	
valid	gültig
validity	Gültigkeit
valuable	wertig
valve	Ventil
vanish	verschwinden
veal	Kalb
ventilation	Belüftung

violation	Verletzung
visual	Bildmaterial
void	unwirksam
voidable	anfechtbar, kündbar
voluntary	freiwillig
volunteer	sich freiwillig melden
w	
wallpaper	Tapete
wardrobe	Kleidung
Whitsun (UK), Pentecost (US)	Pfingsten
wholesaler	Großhändler
willow	Trauerweide
word of mouth	mündlich; hier: mündliche Empfehlung
word processor	Textverarbeitungsprogramm
work in progress	laufende Arbeiten
yellow pages	Gelbe Seiten
z	
ZIP code (US)	Postleitzahl

Images directory – Bildquellenverzeichnis

action press, Hamburg: 24.1 (EVERETT COLLECTION, INC.)
adpic Bildagentur, Bonn: 17.3 (Yuri Arcurs), 69.1 (V. Thoermer)
alamy images, Abingdon/Oxfordshire: 32.3 (grzegorz knec), 34.1, 106.1 (Alex Segre)
allesalltag, Hamburg: 17.2
Cagle Cartoons, Santa Barbara, CA: 44.2
Corbis, Düsseldorf: 5.2 (Rainer Holz), 57.1 (Ocean), 87.1 (Stewart Cohen Pictures/SuperStock)
Coverpicture, Berlin: 69.3 (Robert Kneschke)
die bildstelle, Hamburg: 101.11 (MCPHOTO)
Fotolia Deutschland GmbH, Berlin: 5.3 (endostock), 17.1 (pixelshoot), 32.1, 56.1 (Jan Schuler), 69.2 (coramax), 91.1 (Franz Pfluegl), 101.5 (felinda), 101.7 (Denis Dryashkin)
FotoNatur.de, Ostenfeld: 101.4
Hafen Hamburg Marketing e.V., Hamburg: 60.2
Huwer, Christine, Frankfurt a.M.: 102 (alle)
Imago, Berlin: 60.3
iStockphoto.com, Calgary: 5.1 (Justin Horrocks), 48.1 (LICreate), 101.9 (xxmmxx)
Jochen Tack Fotografie, Essen: 73.1
Naturbildportal, Hannover: 101.12 (Manfred Ruckszio)
Panther Media GmbH, München: 101.6 (Jan Köhl)
Pearson, Carol, Paris: 96.1
Picture-Alliance GmbH, Frankfurt a.M.: 24.2, 44.1, 60.4 (ZB/Nestor Bachmann)
pixelio media GmbH, München: 101.2 (Angelika Lutz)
Reinhard-Tierfoto, Heiligkreuzsteinach: 101.1, 101.3
Sony Music Entertainment Germany GmbH, München: 32.2
transit. fotografie und reportage, Berlin: 60.1 (Tom Schulze), 77.1 (Chr. von Polentz)
Transport for London TfL, London: 99.1
Tönnies, Frauke, Laatzen: 101.8, 101.10
Visum Foto GmbH, Hamburg: 60.9 (Andreas Reeg)

3556134